Chef John's Irish-American Cookbook

Recipes collected over a thirty-five year career in the food service industry, catering to the hungry traveler and worker alike.

Credits

The inspiration for this book has been a lifetime dream and one that I have attempted several times in my Florida retirement — however, our busy life was always interrupted and the project got shelved — however for the past ten years we have made trips to the Emerald Isle and in 1987 we purchased a bungalow in the west of Ireland in a small quaint fishing village called Quilty, County Clare and there met our neighbors Peggy and Martin Morrissey, who were the push to bring my dreams to reality. My gratitude to them and my loving wife for putting up with the clutter and disorganization on two continents.

J. M.

Original type set by
Margaret Torrey
Palm Beach Gardens, Florida

Preface

The Malones live six months of the year in Palm Beach Gardens, Florida on the east coast, approximately one and a half hours north of Miami and three hours south of Orlando. They are active in their church, the cathedral parish of St. Ignatius of Loyola, where John is past Parish Council member, a Eucharistic Minister, and past president of the Ignatius Social Club. They also enjoy growing tropical fruits — ruby red grapefruit, Honey Belle and Hamlin oranges, tangarines-the Dancy variety, also Meyer lemons (thin skin fruit) and Persian Lymes, not to mention avacados, and calamunduns (a cross between lemon and orange, a small round sour fruit, wonderful for jams, pies, cakes, and muffins).

Juanita is active in the Catholic Daughters, past president of the Ignatius Women's Club, and member of the Gardens Womans Club. She pursues a full-time career as a portrait artist; her paintings are presently in ten states and on the continent, both in England and Ireland.

John's father hails from Glendine South Miltown Malbay, County Clare, and John has many relatives residing in and around Clare, as well as Dublin and the continent.

The main objective of this work is to compile many frugal recipes that can be prepared without breaking the budget, and which will perk up the dinner table for your family and guests alike. I have tried from memory to include many recipes that would have universal appeal. I hope you have many happy hours of cooking and experimenting with them.

Good Eating,

J.M.

Published and Printed By
Cookbook Publishers, Inc.
P.O. Box 15920
Lenexa, Kansas 66285-5920

THIS BOOK includes the finest plastic ring binders available, BUT, like most plastics, the BINDERS CAN BE DAMAGED BY EXCESSIVE HEAT, so AVOID exposing them to the direct rays of the SUN, or excessive heat such as IN A CAR on a hot day, or on the top of the kitchen STOVE. If not exposed to heat, the binders will last indefinitely.

TABLE OF CONTENTS

FAVORITE RECIPES
FROM MY COOKBOOK

Recipe Name	Page Number

Starters, Appetizers, Beverages, and Relishes

FOOD QUANTITIES FOR 25, 50, AND 100 SERVINGS

FOOD	25 SERVINGS	50 SERVINGS	100 SERVINGS
Rolls	4 doz.	8 doz.	16 doz.
Bread	50 slices or 3 1-lb. loaves	100 slices or 6 1-lb. loaves	200 slices or 12 1-lb. loaves
Butter	½ lb.	¾ to 1 lb.	1½ lb.
Mayonnaise	1 c.	2 to 3 c.	4 to 6 c.
Mixed filling for sandwiches (meat, eggs, fish)	1½ qt.	2½ to 3 qt.	5 to 6 qt.
Mixed filling (sweet-fruit)	1 qt.	1¾ to 2 qt.	2½ to 4 qt.
Jams & preserves	1½ lb.	3 lb.	6 lb.
Crackers	1½ lb.	3 lb.	6 lb.
Cheese (2 oz. per serving)	3 lb.	6 lb.	12 lb.
Soup	1½ gal.	3 gal.	6 gal.
Salad dressings	1 pt.	2½ pt.	½ gal.
Meat, Poultry, or Fish:			
Wieners (beef)	6½ lb.	13 lb.	25 lb.
Hamburger	9 lb.	18 lb.	35 lb.
Turkey or chicken	13 lb.	25 to 35 lb.	50 to 75 lb.
Fish, large whole (round)	13 lb.	25 lb.	50 lb.
Fish, fillets or steaks	7½ lb.	15 lb.	30 lb.
Salads, Casseroles, Vegetables:			
Potato salad	4¼ qt.	2¼ gal.	4½ gal.
Scalloped potatoes	4½ qt. or 1 12x20" pan	8½ qt.	17 qt.
Mashed potatoes	9 lb.	18-20 lb.	25-35 lb.
Spaghetti	1¼ gal.	2½ gal.	5 gal.
Baked beans	¾ gal.	1¼ gal.	2½ gal.
Jello salad	¾ gal.	1¼ gal.	2½ gal.
Canned vegetables	1 #10 can	2½ #10 cans	4 #10 cans
Fresh Vegetables:			
Lettuce (for salads)	4 heads	8 heads	15 heads
Carrots (3 oz. or ½ c.)	6¼ lb.	12½ lb.	25 lb.
Tomatoes	3-5 lb.	7-10 lb.	14-20 lb.
Desserts:			
Watermelon	37½ lb.	75 lb.	150 lb.
Fruit cup (½ c. per serving)	3 qt.	6 qt.	12 qt.
Cake	1 10x12" sheet cake 1½ 10" layer cakes	1 12x20" sheet cake 3 10" layer cakes	2 12x20" sheet cakes 6 10" layer cakes
Whipping cream	¾ pt.	1½ to 2 pt.	3 pt.
Ice Cream:			
Brick	3¼ qt.	6½ qt.	12½ qt.
Bulk	2¼ qt.	4½ qt. or 1¼ gal.	9 qt. or 2½ gal.
Beverages:			
Coffee	½ lb. and 1½ gal. water	1 lb. and 3 gal. water	2 lb. and 6 gal. water
Tea	1/12 lb. and 1½ gal. water	⅙ lb. and 3 gal. water	⅓ lb. and 6 gal. water
Lemonade	10 to 15 lemons, 1½ gal. water	20 to 30 lemons, 3 gal. water	40 to 60 lemons, 6 gal. water

STARTERS, APPETIZERS, BEVERAGES, AND RELISHES

BACON STUFFED MUSHROOMS

1 lb. fresh mushrooms (about 2 inch diameter)
2 Tbsp. butter or margarine
2 Tbsp. chopped onion
1 slice white bread, chopped fine

1 c. (4 oz.) shredded Cheddar cheese
3 oz. (or more to taste) bacon, cooked and chopped

Wipe mushrooms well with damp cloth. Remove stems from mushrooms and set caps aside. Chop stems and cook with onion in butter until tender. Add bread crumbs and remove from heat. Stir in cheese and bacon bits. Press filling into caps and place in shallow baking pan. Bake at 400°F. for 15 minutes or until cheese is melted. Makes about 18 appetizers.

DEVILED EGGS

12 eggs
1 small can deviled ham

¼ tsp. dry mustard
3 to 4 Tbsp. mayonnaise

Hard cook the eggs. Remove shells and cut lengthwise into halves. Remove the yolks and mash with a fork. Add ham, dry mustard, and mayonnaise (enough to make mixture creamy) to the yolks and mix until smooth. Fill the egg halves with the yolk mixture. Serves 12.

POTATO PANCAKES

They go equally well as appetizer or luncheon entree.

6 large potatoes, peeled and grated with hand grater
1 medium onion, chopped fine
2 large eggs

½ c. flour
1 tsp. salt
1 tsp. nutmeg

Grate potatoes by hand into large bowl. Add finely chopped onion, eggs, flour, salt, nutmeg, and parsley. Mix well by hand. Heat oil in skillet just enough to cover the bottom. Drop tablespoonful of batter into hot oil. Fry on both sides until golden brown. Serve hot with applesauce and/or commercial sour cream.

BAKED PRAWN DIP

2 (8 oz.) pkg. cream cheese
½ c. mayonnaise
2 (6 oz.) pkg. frozen prawns, thawed and diced
2 cloves garlic

4 Tbsp. white wine
2 Tbsp. powdered sugar
1 large bag potato chips or corn chips

Blend all ingredients except chips. Place in a greased baking dish or casserole. Bake, uncovered, in a 350°F. oven for 35 minutes or until bubbly. Frozen crabmeat may be used instead of prawns.

CURRY DIP

1 pt. mayonnaise	¼ tsp. pepper
2 Tbsp. chili sauce	1 Tbsp. grated onion and juice
3 tsp. curry powder	1 tsp. Worcestershire sauce
¼ tsp. salt	

Mix all ingredients and chill. Keeps indefinitely in the refrigerator. Especially good with raw vegetables such as carrots, cauliflower, celery, cucumbers, zucchini, or cherry tomatoes.

BAKED STUFFED CLAMS

I save a few dozen medium size shells from steamed clams. Wash them and keep for this recipe.

¼ c. bread crumbs	2 Tbsp. olive oil
2 cloves garlic, chopped	1 (10½ oz.) can minced clams
1 medium onion, chopped fine	Salt
1 Tbsp. parsley	Parmesan cheese
1 pinch of oregano	

1. Saute first 5 ingredients in olive oil for about 2 minutes, mixing thoroughly. When onion and garlic start to brown, remove from frying pan and mix with clams, juice, salt, and cheese.

2. Spoon into clam shells or bake in shallow ovenware dish. Place on baking sheet in 375° oven for 25 minutes or brown on top.

CLAMS CASINO

Shuck fresh clams, opening with clam knife and leaving clam loosened on half shell. Reserve clams onto baking sheet, allowing 3 or 4 per person.

Topping:

½ c. green pepper, diced	1 lb. bacon, well cooked and
¼ c. red pepper, diced	chopped
¼ c. onion, minced fine	

Saute peppers and onion until tender. Put spoonful of saute mixture onto each clam and pop into oven for a few minutes.

CORN RELISH
(Quick and simple!)

3 (17 oz.) cans whole kernel corn, drained	1 c. chopped green pepper
1½ c. chopped onion	⅓ c. chopped pimento
1 (8 oz.) bottle Catalina French dressing	

Toss ingredients lightly. Chill overnight. Makes 7 cups.

HOT BEEF DIP

1 (8 oz.) pkg. cream cheese
2 Tbsp. milk
1 (2½ oz.) jar or pkg. dried beef
¼ tsp. onion powder

2 Tbsp. finely chopped green
   pepper
½ c. sour cream
¼ c. chopped walnuts

Cream the cheese and milk. Add rest of the ingredients. Put into small greased baking dish and bake at 350°F. for 15 minutes. (Do not overbake.) Serve with crackers.

SAUCY FRANKFURTERS

1½ to 2 lb. frankfurters
¾ of 1 small jar prepared mustard

1 (12 oz.) jar red currant jelly

Beat mustard and jelly until blended in double boiler. Cut frankfurters into 1 inch pieces and heat. Add to sauce and simmer for 30 minutes. Keep warm in fondue dish for serving.

IMPOSSIBLE QUICHE

3 eggs
½ c. flour
6 Tbsp. melted butter
1½ c. milk

¼ tsp. salt plus pepper
1 c. shredded Swiss cheese
½ c. diced ham

Mix all ingredients, except ham and cheese, in a blender or food processor for 30 seconds. Pour into greased 9 inch pie plate. Sprinkle ham and cheese evenly over the top and press down into the egg mixture. Bake at 350°F. for 45 minutes. Let stand for 5 to 10 minutes before cutting.

CHEESE BALL

1 (8 oz.) soft Cheddar cheese
1 (8 oz.) cream cheese
1 tsp. finely chopped onion or onion
   powder

1 tsp. dry parsley
Chopped nuts

Soften cheeses for several hours and mix well together. Add and mix in onion and parsley. Form into ball and place in refrigerator for 1 hour. Roll in chopped nuts. Keep refrigerated until ready to serve.

LIPTON VEGETABLE DIP

1 env. Lipton vegetable recipe soup
   mix

1 pt. (16 oz.) commercial sour cream

In small bowl, blend ingredients. Chill at least 2 hours. Makes 2 cups.

Dip variation:

Use French onion mix instead of vegetable.

Add to the vegetable dip 10 ounce package frozen chopped spinach thawed and squeezed dry.

CHAMPAGNE MUSTARD

⅔ c. white champagne vinegar
⅔ c. dry mustard, sifted (small tin is enough)

3 eggs
1 c. sugar

Mix together the vinegar and mustard. Beat eggs and sugar. Add egg and sugar mixture to mustard mixture and cook in top of double boiler over boiling water until thick. Refrigerate.

BAKED COLD LIMERICK HAM AND MELON

1 to 2 honeydew or Spanish melons
1 lb. ham, sliced thin

Freshly ground pepper

Cut the melon in half. Cut off the rind and slice the melon in crescent shape strips. Alternate slices of melon and sliced ham (thin) on cold plates. Sprinkle with ground fresh black pepper.

DRUNKEN CHICKEN LIVERS

½ lb. chicken livers
⅓ c. finely chopped onions
⅜ c. butter
1½ oz. bourbon or whiskey
1 tsp. lemon juice
¼ tsp. Worcestershire sauce

2 tsp. prepared mustard (Dijon)
½ tsp. dry mustard
2 Tbsp. heavy cream
1 tsp. horseradish
½ tsp. salt
⅛ tsp. fresh ground pepper

Saute livers and onions in butter. Add whiskey. When hot, set ablaze for about 10 seconds. Continue to saute slowly about 8 or 10 minutes, then blend in electric blender with the remaining ingredients. Store overnight in refrigerator. Serve as canape with crackers or toast, sieved egg, and parsley.

DEVILED EGG SAIL BOATS

Bring 6 eggs to boil. Cook 20 minutes. Run cold water over them and crack shell to make peeling easy. Cut in two lengthwise. In a bowl, mash the yolks with enough mayonnaise to make them thick and creamy. Add ¼ teaspoon salt and a pinch of garlic salt or curry. Whip with fork. Fill shells. Sprinkle with paprika. Make sails. Cut from red and green peppers. Run a toothpick through them for a mast and stick into the eggs. Alternate red and green sails for a nice effect.

ONION PANCAKES

1 c. flour
1 tsp. baking powder
2 eggs

1 c. milk
½ c. water
1 large onion

Cut onion fine. Fry in butter at low heat for 10 minutes. Mix other ingredients well and beat for 5 minutes. Add onion to batter and beat 5 minutes more. Fry in oil until golden brown on both sides. Serve with meats of all kinds. Great for evening tea with leftover cold bacon, ham, roast pork, chicken, etc.

4

HUMUS

A wonderful spread instead of butter or dairy spread.

2 c. chickpeas or garbanzos
⅔ c. Taheeni
1 Tbsp. lemon juice
¾ c. chicken stock

½ c. garlic cloves
Parsley, chopped
Black olives

Puree chickpeas, Taheeni, lemon juice, chicken stock, and garlic. Garnish with fresh chopped parsley and black olives. Yields 3 cups.

This dip should be made 24 hours before serving and stored refrigerated.

For Taheeni:

4 Tbsp. ground sesame seeds,
    ground in mortar

1 tsp. sesame oil
1 Tbsp. lemon juice

ROQUEFORT OR BLUE CHEESE MOUSSE

¼ lb. Roquefort cheese
1 env. unflavored gelatin
¼ c. lemon juice
1 c. grated cucumber, drained
4 Tbsp. minced parsley
2 Tbsp. minced pimento

1 Tbsp. minced capers
1 tsp. grated onion
1 tsp. salt
½ tsp. ground pepper
1 c. heavy cream, whipped

Soften gelatin in lemon juice; add 1 cup boiling water and stir until gelatin is dissolved. Mash cheese. Add remaining ingredients except cream. Mix well. Combine with gelatin mixture. Chill for 20 minutes or until mixture is slightly thickened. Fold in whipped cream. Pour into mold and chill 4 hours. Serves 6.

Compliment with a good champagne. For a different starter, serve on leaf of lettuce with crackers or toast points.

BLEU CHEESE BALL

½ lb. cream cheese
¼ lb. Bleu cheese
1 (14 oz.) can black olives, pitted
    and chopped

½ c. chopped walnuts
2 Tbsp. butter or margarine

Bring cheese and butter to room temperature. Mix thoroughly and add olives. Form into ball and roll in chopped nuts. Refrigerate for at least 2 hours before serving. May be made several days in advance.

SALMON BALL

1 (No. 1) can red salmon
1 (8 oz.) pkg. cream cheese
1 Tbsp. lemon
1 tsp. horseradish
2 tsp. grated onion

¼ tsp. salt
⅛ tsp. Tabasco sauce
½ c. chopped walnuts
3 Tbsp. minced parsley

Soften the cream cheese. Drain and flake the salmon, discarding any bony pieces and skin. Mix these 2 together, beating well. Add the lemon juice, horseradish, onion, salt, and Tabasco sauce. Chill for 4 hours. Form into ball and roll in chopped nuts and minced parsley. Chill again. Serves 12.

HOT CHOCOLATE

For 10 or 12.

6 sq. Baker's chocolate
1 c. water
6 Tbsp. sugar
8 c. rich milk

1 c. cream, whipped
1 Tbsp. brandy, 2 tsp. vanilla, or 2 tsp. instant coffee

Melt the chocolate and water in double boiler. When melted and smooth, add sugar gradually, stirring all the time. Scald milk. Do not let it boil and pour onto chocolate mixture, beating well with wire whisk. Add flavoring. Keep beating until it froths. Serve whipped cream on side.

COFFEE DRINK

Half fill a tall glass of mug with hot coffee. Add a spoonful of ice cream and a jigger of brandy.

COFFEE MILK PUNCH

In large crystal punch bowl, put:

3 qt. cold strong coffee
2½ gal. coffee ice cream (whole)

1 c. rum or brandy
2 pt. whipped cream

Fold all together and ladle out into glass coffee punch cups.

Breads, Rolls, Glendine-Breakfast, and Toast Dishes

MICROWAVE HINTS

1. Place an open box of hardened brown sugar in the microwave oven with 1 cup hot water. Microwave at high for 1½ to 2 minutes for ½ pound or 2 to 3 minutes for 1 pound.
2. Soften hard ice cream by microwaving at 30% power. One pint will take 15 to 30 seconds; one quart, 30 to 45 seconds; and one-half gallon, 45 seconds to one minute.
3. One stick of butter or margarine will soften in 1 minute when microwaved at 20% power.
4. Soften one 8-ounce package of cream cheese by microwaving at 30% power for 2 to 2½ minutes. One 3-ounce package of cream cheese will soften in 1½ to 2 minutes.
5. Thaw frozen orange juice right in the container. Remove the top metal lid. Place the opened container in the microwave and heat on high power 30 seconds for 6 ounces and 45 seconds for 12 ounces.
6. Thaw whipped topping...a 4½ ounce carton will thaw in 1 minute on the defrost setting. Whipped topping should be slightly firm in the center but it will blend well when stirred. Do not overthaw!
7. Soften jello that has set up too hard - perhaps you were to chill it until slightly thickened and forgot it. Heat on a low power setting for a very short time.
8. Dissolve gelatin in the microwave. Measure liquid in a measuring cup, add jello and heat. There will be less stirring to dissolve the gelatin.
9. Heat hot packs in a microwave oven. A wet fingertip towel will take about 25 seconds. It depends on the temperature of the water used to wet the towel.
10. To scald milk, cook 1 cup milk for 2-2½ minutes, stirring once each minute.
11. To make dry bread crumbs, cut 6 slices bread into ½-inch cubes. Microwave in 3-quart casserole 6-7 minutes, or until dry, stirring after 3 minutes. Crush in blender.
12. Refresh stale potato chips, crackers, or other snacks of such type by putting a plateful in the microwave oven for about 30-45 seconds. Let stand for 1 minute to crisp. Cereals can also be crisped.
13. Melt almond bark for candy or dipping pretzels. One pound will take about 2 minutes, stirring twice. If it hardens while dipping candy, microwave for a few seconds longer.
14. Nuts will be easier to shell if you place 2 cups of nuts in a 1-quart casserole with 1 cup of water. Cook for 4 to 5 minutes and the nut meats will slip out whole after cracking the shell.
15. When thawing hamburger meat, the outside will many times begin cooking before the meat is completely thawed. Defrost for 3 minutes, then remove the outside portions that have defrosted. Continue defrosting the hamburger, taking off the defrosted outside portions at short intervals.
16. To drain the fat from hamburger while it is cooking in the microwave oven (one pound cooks in 5 minutes on high), cook it in a plastic colander placed inside a casserole dish.
17. Cubed meat and chopped vegetables will cook more evenly if cut uniformly.
18. When baking large cakes, brownies, or moist bars, place a juice glass in the center of the baking dish to prevent a soggy middle and ensure uniform baking throughout.
19. Since cakes and quick breads rise higher in a microwave oven, fill pans just half full of batter.
20. For stamp collectors: Place a few drops of water on stamp to be removed from envelope. Heat in the microwave for 20 seconds and the stamp will come right off.
21. Using a round dish instead of a square one eliminates overcooked corners in baking cakes.
22. When preparing chicken in a dish, place meaty pieces around the edges and the bony pieces in the center of the dish.
23. Shaping meatloaf into a ring eliminates undercooked center. A glass set in the center of a dish can serve as the mold.
24. Treat fresh meat cuts for 15 to 20 seconds on high in the microwave oven. This cuts down on meat-spoiling types of bacteria.
25. A crusty coating of chopped walnuts surrounding many microwave-cooked cakes and quick breads enhances the looks and eating quality. Sprinkle a layer of medium finely chopped walnuts evenly onto the bottom and sides of a ring pan or Bundt cake pan. Pour in batter and microwave as recipe directs.
26. Do not salt foods on the surface as it causes dehydration (meats and vegetables) and toughens the food. Salt the meat after you remove it from the oven unless the recipe calls for using salt in the mixture.
27. Heat leftover custard and use it as frosting for a cake.
28. Melt marshmallow creme in the microwave oven. Half of a 7-ounce jar will melt in 35-40 seconds on high. Stir to blend.
29. Toast coconut in the microwave. Watch closely because it browns quickly once it begins to brown. Spread ½ cup coconut in a pie plate and cook for 3-4 minutes, stirring every 30 seconds after 2 minutes.
30. Place a cake dish up on another dish or on a roasting rack if you have difficulty getting the bottom of the cake done. This also works for potatoes and other foods that don't quite get done on the bottom.

BREADS, ROLLS, GLENDINE -
BREAKFAST, AND TOAST DISHES

In Glendine, Miltown Malbay Co. Clare Baking Day was literally a day dedicated to baking as this chore was done on the open fire or in a small oven placed near the coals or on the griddle for griddle cakes, bread, or scones. For those lucky enough to have a brick oven, a fire had to be started, usually with brush wood and on top, larger wood to make a solid fire. As the wood burned, large logs were put in the door, securely closed, and logs left to burn until reduced to glowing ash. They were then spread evenly throughout the whole floor as for even heat. This operation would take nearly 2 hours, so it's not surprising that having gotten the oven hot the fullest use was made of it.

Baking the weeks batch of bread and tarts and heat lowering, then the treacle cakes, tea bracks, fruit cake, and biscuits, and in the last heat, drying out bread crumbs and herbs. The advent of the coal fired solid fuel cooker must have been a miracle to the Irish farmer's wife, but people that remember bread baked in the old brick oven say that no bread today tastes the same. I remember at about 13 or 14 years being on a weekend Scout camping trip to Winsted, Connecticut, "Camp Sequassen," baking my first pie, a deep dish peach in an old stone fireplace oven. This took almost 12 hours because of down drafts, etc., but it was the best tasting pie I ever baked. It had a "nutty" oven taste. This we do not get today with our modern gas or electric ranges.

I cook on a large commercial Vulcan American range with 2 ovens, 6 gas burners, a grill top, and broiler under at Spanish Point and this stove produces breads better than any bakery bread. They are superior in taste and goodness. We can now be sure to have the correct degree of heat, be it Fahrenheit or Celsius, and once our baking is in the oven, it looks after itself with much better results than its tired, dirty ancestor, "the coal or solid fuel cooker."

My experience has been that you need a very hot oven for good soda breads, be it wheeten or white, 450°F. in my gas range in Ireland and also 450°F. in my electric oven in Palm Beach Gardens, Florida. This produces a nice crusty light textured bread, ideal for breakfast, with soup, or anytime with a cuppa. Nothing compares to the aroma of freshly baked bread, especially if it's your own freshly baked bread.

SODA BREAD NUMBER 1

4 c. white flour
1 tsp. salt
1 tsp. baking soda

2 c. buttermilk or sour milk
2 Tbsp. butter or oleo

SODA BREAD NUMBER 2

4 c. white flour
1 Tbsp. oleo
1 tsp. baking soda

1 c. buttermilk or sweet milk
1 tsp. salt

Sieve the dry ingredients into a large bowl. Aerate the mixture by scooping up handfuls and letting it fall through your fingers. Add enough buttermilk to make a soft dough, working quickly as the buttermilk and soda are now reacting. Too much handling will toughen it. Form a round loaf as thick as your fist. Cut a cross with the back of your hand dipped in flour. Bake on floured baking sheet at 450°F. for 35 to 40 minutes. When baked, the loaf will sound hollow with a tap on the bottom.

Variation: Wheaten Soda Bread is made the same way with whole meal flour replacing all or some of the white flour. Also use less buttermilk.

SODA BREAD NUMBER 3
(Wheeten style)

2 c. white flour
2 c. wheat flour
1 fistful wheat germ
¼ c. wheat bran

1 tsp. salt
1 tsp. baking powder
2 Tbsp. oleo
2 + c. buttermilk

IRISH RAISIN SODA BREAD

4 c. sifted flour
½ c. granulated sugar
¼ c. shortening
1 tsp. baking powder
1 c. currants or raisins

2 Tbsp. caraway seeds
1 egg
1 tsp. baking soda
1⅓ c. sour milk or buttermilk

Mix together egg, baking soda, and milk, then mix this with the flour, sugar, shortening, baking powder, raisins, and caraway seeds. Knead lightly (until smooth). Bake in a round shape at about 350°F. to 375°F. for an hour.

DINGLE LOAF SODA BREAD

One loaf:

10 oz. whole meal flour
5½ oz. white flour
¾ oz. brown sugar
½ tsp. soda
1 oz. bran wheat
1 oz. wheat germ

1 tsp. salt
1 tsp. sunflower oil
¾ pt. milk
1 egg
Little butter

Four loaves:

40 oz. whole meal flour
22 oz. white flour
3 oz. brown sugar
2 tsp. soda
4 oz. bran wheat
4 oz. wheat germ

3 tsp. salt
4 tsp. sunflower oil
3 pt. milk
4 eggs
Little butter

In mixing bowl, measure out whole meal flour, white flour, brown sugar, soda, bran wheat, wheat germ, and salt and work, blending with fingers. In blender swirl oil, milk, egg, and melted butter. Add to dry ingredients. Mix and put in buttered loaf pan. Bake at 400°F. for approximately 1 hour.

WHOLE MEAL LOAF

Exquisitely simple and delicious to eat.

1 lb. Hearts Delight wheaten meal	1 c. milk
½ lb. Odlums coarse ground whole	1 tsp. salt
meal	2 Tbsp. cooking oil
4 oz. Odlums cream flour	Wheat
½ pt. buttermilk	Wheat germ
2 tsp. bread soda	

Mix whole wheat, wheaten meal, cream flour, bread soda, and salt together in a bowl. Add the buttermilk, milk, and oil. After stirring all of the ingredients well, pour the mixture into 2 greased 2 pound loaf tins. Bake in preheated oven at 350° for approximately 1½ hours. Cool on a wire rack.

SCONES IDEAL ANY TIME

Scones are great at coffee time, tea time, supper time, and picnic time. In fact, they are great anytime. They are an ideal standby in the freezer because they can be topped with almost anything. To serve the unexpected visitor, I make a batch of brown "wheeten" scones, cutting them into large triangles which can be slit and used for open face sandwiches. Topped with a slice of cheese and pickles or served with a bowl of homemade soup, they make a quick sustaining lunch.

Shredded lettuce, tomatoes, coleslaw, and cold meat such as chicken, turkey, or ham, tuna or tinned salmon mixed with chopped onion and mayonnaise, cream cheese topped with cucumber, apple, or chutney are just a few suggestions for toppings. Let your leftovers in the fridge guide you along. (Fruit scones or wheeten made with self-rising flour or whole meal self-rising flour.) I use brown sugar yogurt, sour milk, buttermilk, whatever happens to be in the fridge.

CHEESE AND BACON SCONES

8 oz. self-rising flour	2 oz. soft tub margarine
2 level tsp. baking powder	3 oz. grated Cheddar cheese
½ level tsp. dry mustard	3 rashers of bacon, cooked and
¼ level tsp. salt	finely chopped
Pinch of pepper	6 to 7 Tbsp. milk

To glaze, use beaten egg yolk. Oven temperature 425°F./220°C./gas 7.

COTTAGE CHEESE SCONES

8 oz. self-rising flour	3 oz. cottage cheese
Pinch of salt	1 egg
2 oz. butter	¼ pt. milk

Oven temperature 450°F./230°C./gas 8. Sieve the flour and salt into a bowl. Rub in the butter, then mix in the cheese and beaten egg. Add milk gradually until a smooth dough is formed. Roll out and cut into shapes. Place on a baking sheet. Brush the tops with milk and bake in a preheated hot oven for 12 to 15 minutes.

Scones are great on their own or with butter, jam, marmalade, clotted cream, or honey. Irish honey is the best. The Bogne Valley, Drogheda, Co. Louth is famous for its honey manufacturing. Ireland has many small farmers making honey from clover or other special flowers in their local. These may be found in craft shoppes, specialty shoppes, or health food stores around the countryside. The flavors differ greatly when bees are with clovers, gorse, heathers, etc.

CHEESE AND BACON SCONES

Sieve the flour, baking powder, mustard, and salt and pepper together into a bowl. Add all the other ingredients and mix together thoroughly with a wooden spoon to form a dough. Turn out onto a lightly floured board. Roll to a ½ inch thickness and cut into rounds. Place on baking sheet and brush tops with beaten egg yolk. Bake in a preheated oven for 12 to 15 minutes. Remove from oven and cool on a wire tray.

Note: If you don't have soft margarine, rub in the margarine or butter with the tips of your fingers (or buzz the flour, etc., in the food processor with the margarine or butter and then add rest of ingredients.

WHOLE MEAL CHEESE SCONES

1 lb. whole meal flour (Odlums or other)
2 tsp. baking powder
1 Tbsp. fresh mixed herbs, chopped

5 oz. margarine
4 oz. grated mature Cheddar cheese
½ pt. milk

Oven temperature 425°F./220°C./gas 7. Mix together the flour, baking powder, and herbs. Rub in the margarine until the mixture resembles bread crumbs. Add most of the grated cheese, leaving about 1 tablespoon. Using a knife, gradually mix in the milk until you have a soft dough. Knead lightly with your hands. Roll out the dough on a floured surface to ¾ inch thick and cut into rounds using a 2¼ inch cutter. Place the scones on a greased baking sheet. Brush with a little milk, then sprinkle with remaining cheese over the top. Bake 15 to 20 minutes.

YOGURT SCONES

8 oz. whole meal flour
½ tsp. salt
½ tsp. baking powder
2 oz. polyunsaturated margarine

1 Tbsp. brown sugar
¼ pt. lowfat natural yogurt
Milk for glazing
Sesame seeds for sprinkling

Oven temperature 220°C./425°F./gas 7.Sift the flour, salt, and baking powder into a bowl, tipping in any bran left in the sieve. Rub in the fat until the mixture resembles bread crumbs, then stir in the sugar. Add the yogurt and mix to a soft dough. Turn onto a floured surface. Knead lightly and roll out to a ¾ inch thickness. Cut into 2 inch rounds with a fluted cutter and place on a floured baking sheet. Brush with milk. Sprinkle with sesame seeds and bake in a preheated hot oven for 12 to 15 minutes. Transfer to a wire rack to cool.

Variations:

Cheese and Sesame Scones: Sift in 1 teaspoon dry mustard and pinch of cayenne pepper with the baking powder. Replace the sugar with 3 ounces grated lowfat cheese and 1 tablespoon of sesame seeds.

Date Nut Scones: Sift in ½ teaspoon ground cinnamon with the baking powder. Mix in 1 ounce chopped dates and 1 ounce chopped walnuts with the sugar.

BUTTERMILK BISCUITS

Popular in the U.S.A. Serve with jam or marmalade or split and covered with strawberries topped with cream.

2 c. white flour	¾ tsp. salt
2 tsp. baking powder	¼ c. shortening
¼ tsp. soda	1 c. buttermilk (approx.)

Preheat oven to 450°F. Sift together flour, baking powder, soda, and salt. Cut in shortening with pastry blender or 2 knives until mixture is consistency of coarse crumbs. Add buttermilk and stir with fork just until dough leaves sides of bowl. Turn out onto lightly floured board. Knead gently just until smooth. Roll out to ½ inch thickness. Cut with floured 2 inch cutter. Place on baking sheet. Bake 10 to 12 minutes or until golden brown. Makes 12 to 14 biscuits.

Note: To make biscuits using regular milk, follow the recipe preceding, omitting soda. Increase baking soda to 3 teaspoons and use about ¾ cup regular milk.

SCONES NUMBER 1

2 c. self-rising flour	2 Tbsp. sugar
3 Tbsp. butter	Pinch of salt
1½ c. milk	

Sieve flour into bowl and rub in the butter quickly with fingers. Add salt and mix in milk a little at a time. Knead softly, adding more milk if necessary. Roll on floured board and cut out with pastry cutter. Cook on a greased cookie sheet in preheated oven at 425°F. for 12 to 15 minutes.

Note: For brown scones, substitute whole meal flour for ½ the white flour. For fruit scones, add 1 tablespoon of Caster sugar and a fistful of dried fruit before adding the milk.

SCONES NUMBER 2

2 c. flour	¼ tsp. bread soda
2 oz. butter	Pinch of salt
2 Tbsp. baking powder	1 egg (optional)
1 Tbsp. sugar	Sultanas or raisins
½ c. sour or regular milk	

Sieve flour, salt, and soda together into a large bowl. Cut in butter and rub in until like crumbs. Add sugar and enough milk to make a soft dough together with 1 beaten egg. Turn onto floured board. Lightly knead a few times. Roll out and cut into round cakes about 2x1 inch or diamond shape. Bake in hot oven (about 400°F.) for 25 minutes or until scones have risen and are nicely browned. Makes 12.

PLAIN MUFFINS

2 c. sifted flour	1 c. milk
½ tsp. salt	1 egg
1 Tbsp. sugar	2 Tbsp. shortening
4 tsp. baking powder	

Sift flour, salt, sugar, and baking powder together. Combine remaining ingredients and add to the dry ingredients. Stir enough to dampen the flour. Pour into greased pans, filling them ⅔ full. Bake in hot oven at 425°F. for 20 to 25 minutes. Makes 12.

For pineapple muffins: Add ½ cup flour, 3 tablespoons sugar, 2 tablespoons more of shortening, and 1 can (No. 1) crushed and drained pineapple. Mix and bake as preceding.

OATMEAL MUFFINS

¾ c. sifted flour
2 tsp. baking powder
¾ tsp. salt
⅓ c. sugar

1 c. oatmeal (quick cook)
¼ c. margarine
2 eggs, lightly beaten
½ c. milk

Topping:

1 Tbsp. melted oleo

¼ c. quick cooking oatmeal

Sift flour, baking powder, salt, and sugar together. Add oatmeal. Melt margarine and add to mixture. Add eggs and milk. Mix well and put into greased muffin pans. Mix melted oleo and oatmeal and place on top of muffins. Bake at 400°F. for 20 to 30 minutes.

NUTMEG MUFFINS

2 c. flour
1½ c. brown sugar
¾ c. butter or margarine
1 c. flour
2 tsp. baking powder

2 tsp. nutmeg
½ tsp. baking soda
½ tsp. salt
1 c. buttermilk
2 eggs, slightly beaten

Mix 2 cups flour and the brown sugar in medium size bowl. Cut in butter with 2 knives or pastry blender until mixture resembles coarse corn meal. Reserve ¾ cup of the mixture for the topping.

Add 1 cup flour, the baking powder, nutmeg, baking soda, and salt to remaining mixture in the bowl. Add buttermilk and eggs, stirring just until moistened. Spoon into well greased muffin pans, filling ½ full. Sprinkle each muffin with 1½ teaspoons of topping. Bake at 350°F. for 20 to 25 minutes. Makes 2 dozen.

BRAN MUFFINS

¾ c. white flour
¾ c. whole wheat flour
¼ c. sugar
2 tsp. baking powder
¼ tsp. salt

¼ tsp. cinnamon
2 c. bran flakes cereal
1¼ c. milk
¼ c. oil
1 egg, slightly beaten

Heat oven to 400°F. and grease 12 muffin tins. Lightly spoon flour into measuring cup; level off in small bowl. Combine both flours, sugar, baking powder, salt, and cinnamon. Mix well and set aside. In large bowl, combine cereal and milk. Let stand for 3 minutes. Add oil and egg, blending well. Add flour mixture to cereal mixture. Stir until dry ingredients are moistened. Fill greased muffin tins ⅔ full. Bake at 400°F. for 15 to 20 minutes or until lightly browned. Serve warm. Makes 12.

Method No. 2:

This batter may be refrigerated in a plastic container with tight cover for up to 2 weeks and used in small quantities whenever needed.

Place ½ cup of salad oil in mixing bowl with ¾ cup of sugar. Beat until blended. Add 2 eggs and beat well. Measure 2½ cups flour (I use unbleached). Add ½ teaspoon salt and 2½ teaspoons baking soda. Add this alternately to preceding mixture with 2 cups of buttermilk. Pour cup of boiling water over 1 cup raisins, 2 cups Kellogg's All-Bran, and 1 cup Nabisco Bran. When cooled a bit, add to flour-oil mixture. Bake at 400°F. for 20 minutes. Makes 36.

LO-FAT BRAN MUFFINS

4 c. flour	5 c. milk
8 tsp. baking powder	1⅓ c. brown sugar
2 tsp. baking soda	4 eggs
2 tsp. cinnamon	2 c. applesauce
8 c. 100% bran	

Mix the flour, baking powder, baking soda, cinnamon, and bran. Add milk, brown sugar, eggs, and applesauce, mixing all ingredients well. Bake at 400°F. for 20 to 25 minutes.

BRACK

A favorite of my Irish family and guests alike.

Steep overnight ¾ cup mixed fruit and a cup of brown sugar in a cup of strong tea. (We save all the tea from the bottom of the pot.) Next morning, add 1 beaten egg, 2 cups self-rising flour, and a pinch of salt. Add cherries, mixed peel, or walnuts if you like. Bake at 325° to 350°F. for 45 minutes.

ZUCCHINI BREAD
(Courgettes Bread)

4 eggs	1 tsp. cinnamon
2 c. sugar	2 c. zucchini, grated
1 c. oil	1 c. raisins or dates
3½ c. flour	1 c. granola or nuts
1½ tsp. baking soda	1 tsp. vanilla
1½ tsp. salt	

Mix all of the preceding ingredients together. Place in a greased Bundt cake pan. Bake at 350°F. for 50 to 60 minutes.

ANA DAMA BREAD

½ c. corn meal	1 pkg. dry yeast or 1 compressed
3 Tbsp. shortening	¼ c. warm water
¼ c. molasses	1 egg, beaten
1 tsp. salt	3 c. sifted flour
¾ c. boiling water	

Combine corn meal, shortening, molasses, salt, and boiling water in large bowl. Let stand until lukewarm. Sprinkle yeast over warm water to dissolve, then stir ½ flour into the corn meal mixture. Beat vigorously. Stir in rest of flour and into a soft ball. Transfer to greased loaf pan and cover with cloth. Let rise in warm place until 1 inch above pan. Sprinkle with corn meal and bake in preheated oven at 350°F. for 50 to 55 minutes.

BREAKFAST BREAD

Keeps well and makes wonderful toast.

2 c. buttermilk
½ c. honey
¼ c. molasses
2 tsp. baking soda
½ tsp. salt

1½ c. whole wheat flour
½ c. wheat germ or bran
1 c. white flour
½ c. raisins

Mix together buttermilk, honey, molasses, soda, and salt. In another bowl, combine wheat, white flours, and bran. Add that to the buttermilk mixture. Stir in raisins and pour batter into a 9x5x3 inch loaf pan. Preheat oven to 400°F. and reduce heat to 350°F. when placing pan in oven. Bake for 1 hour.

DATE NUT BREAD

1 tsp. baking soda
1 c. boiling water
1 c. pitted dates, cut up
¾ c. raisins
2 Tbsp. soft butter

1 c. sugar
1 tsp. vanilla extract
1 egg
1⅓ c. flour
¾ c. chopped pecans

Pour soda and boiling water over dates and raisins. Set aside. Cream butter and sugar. Add vanilla and then add egg. Beat well. Add flour and mix well. Pour in fruit mixture including water and add pecans. Mix well again. Bake in buttered 9x5 inch loaf pan at 350°F. for 1 hour and 10 minutes.

POPPY SEED BREAD

3 beaten eggs
1¾ c. sugar
1½ c. milk
1½ c. oil
3 c. flour

1½ tsp. salt
1½ tsp. baking powder
1½ tsp. almond flavor
1½ tsp. vanilla
1½ Tbsp. poppy seed

Glaze:

¾ c. powdered sugar
¼ c. orange juice

½ tsp. vanilla
½ tsp. almond flavor

Sift dry ingredients, except for poppy seeds, into bowl, then mix with liquid ingredients and poppy seeds. Pour into 2 greased and floured 9x4x3 inch loaf pans. Bake at 350°F. for 50 to 60 minutes. Cool for 3 to 5 minutes, then remove to cooling rack.

Glaze: Mix all glaze ingredients. Stir until smooth. Glaze bread while still warm.

LEMON BREAD

May also use limes instead of lemons.

1 c. sugar
⅓ c. melted butter or oleo
1 Tbsp. lemon extract or juice of ½
   lemon
2 eggs (unbeaten)
1½ c. sifted flour

1 tsp. baking powder
1 tsp. salt
½ c. milk
Grated peel of large lemon or lime
½ c. chopped pecans

Beat together sugar, melted butter, and lemon, then beat in eggs. Sift together dry ingredients and add alternating with milk to egg mixture. Beat and blend. Fold in lemon peel and nuts. Turn into 1 large or 2 small greased pans. Bake at 350°F., 1 hour.

Topping:

Juice of 1 large lemon

⅓ c. sugar

Blend until smooth. Heat until melted. Drizzle over warm loaf.

PINEAPPLE BREAD

1¾ c. flour
1½ tsp. soda
½ tsp. salt

½ tsp. ginger
½ tsp. cinnamon
¼ tsp. cloves

Beat 1 egg with ½ cup margarine. Add ⅔ cup of light molasses. Heat 1 (8 ounce) can of crushed pineapple, not drained. Add to eggs and stir. Add dry ingredients. Bake at 375°F. for 25 minutes.

IRISH OATMEAL BREAD WITH SWEET BUTTER

This smells great while cooking and tastes even better. Make this and freeze; wrap securely in aluminum foil and reheat in oven. Have tub of sweet butter on your serving table or spread it on ahead of time. Easily prepared. Makes 2 loaves.

3 c. sifted flour
1¼ c. quick cooking rolled oats
1½ Tbsp. baking powder
1 Tbsp. salt

½ c. honey
1½ c. milk
1 Tbsp. melted butter
1 egg, beaten

Preheat oven to 350°F. Mix first 4 ingredients. In another bowl, add honey, milk, and butter to the beaten egg. Pour egg mixture into oat mixture, stirring until dry ingredients are moistened. Mixture will be lumpy. Spread into 2 greased and floured loaf pans. Bake 1 hour. Turn out of pans onto a wire rack.

DROP SCONES - PANCAKES

2 c. plain flour
½ tsp. baking soda
½ tsp. salt

2 tsp. sugar
1 large egg
1 c. buttermilk

Sift dry ingredients into bowl. Make a well in the middle with a wooden spoon and add the egg. Break the yolk and pour in the buttermilk, mixing quickly to a thick batter. Do not beat as this would develop the gluten in the flour and make the cakes go flat. Fry in large dollops on a lightly greased hot griddle or heavy frying pan. Drop scones are best served hot for tea. Spread them with melting butter and syrup or jam.

ORANGE BREAD

From my Grandmother Stowell's collection. She was born in 1876 in Windham, Vermont.

¾ c. sugar
4 c. flour
4 tsp. baking powder
⅛ tsp. salt

1 egg
2 c. milk
1 Tbsp. melted butter

Put 2 or 3 orange peels with membrane removed in the food processor or hand grinder to give about 1 cup full of ground peel. Add 1 cup sugar and 1 cup water and boil until quite thick. Sift dry ingredients together. In a separate bowl, beat lightly egg, milk, and melted butter. Add to dry ingredients with hot orange mixture. Bake at 350°F. for 45 minutes. Makes 2 loaves.

DATE NUT BREAD NUMBER 2

Cut up 1 box of pitted dates and pour over this 1 cup boiling water, then in separate bowl beat up 2 eggs and 1½ cups sugar and then sift together 3 cups flour, 1 teaspoon baking powder, and ½ teaspoon salt. Put that and egg mixture together with date mixture. Add 1 cup chopped nuts. Fold into a greased and floured loaf pan. Bake at 350°, 1 hour. Yield: 1 loaf.

SOUR CREAM GRAHAM BREAD

For 2 loaves:

2 c. white flour
2 c. graham flour
1 tsp. salt
2 tsp. baking soda
2 tsp. baking powder

2 eggs, well beaten
½ c. thick sour cream
1½ c. sour milk
1⅓ c. maple syrup or Treceal syrup

Sift dry ingredients. Beat the eggs well and stir them into the cream, milk, and syrup. The batter should be quite stiff. Add a little more graham flour if necessary. Butter bread tins and line them with waxed paper. Fill ⅔ full with mixture. Bake in moderately hot oven, 375° for ½ hour. Change position of pans in oven. Reduce to 350° and bake ½ hour longer. Test with straw.

BISHOPS BREAD

½ c. soft butter
1 c. light or dark brown sugar, firmly
   packed
2 eggs

1 c. milk
2¾ c. flour
3 tsp. baking powder
1 tsp. salt

16

Topping:

½ c. white sugar   1 Tbsp. cinnamon
½ c. flour   ½ c. chopped nuts (optional)
¼ c. soft butter

Cream butter, sugar, and eggs until light and fluffy. Blend in the milk all at once. Add sifted dry ingredients. Beat just to combine. Spread in greased and floured pan, 13x9x2 inches. Add topping which has been mixed to the crumbly stage and bake at 375° for 25 to 35 minutes.

BISHOPS BREAD NUMBER 2

1¼ c. sifted flour   3 eggs
1 c. sugar   1 c. walnuts, chopped
1½ tsp. baking powder   ⅔ c. semi-sweet chocolate bits
¼ tsp. salt   1 c. snipped dates
¼ c. soft margarine   1 c. candied cherries

Sift flour, baking powder, and salt in bowl. Mix in fruits and nuts in large bowl. Beat eggs and add sugar and butter. Fold into flour mixture. Grease well and flour a loaf pan. Bake at 325° for 1½ hours.

GLENDINE

The family ancestral farm house in the Malone family for over 250 years (now owned by a first cousin and his wife) can boast a hatchery with over a thousand laying hens. We are supplied with free range eggs for our table twice weekly from Mary herself, my cousin's wife. I fondly remember my first visit to Glendine in 1957 and Uncle Mick's wife Mary also grabbed hold of one of the roosters, wrung its neck, and had it into the huge iron pot on the turf fire. In no time she had a wonderful stewed dinner on the table with farm fresh produce. This rare breed of woman are gone today with working moms and the microwave.

TEA - BREWING METHOD

Good tea must be made in pottery, ceramic, or stainless steel. Boil water in electric teakettle. Heat pot with hot water and toss out. Put 1 teaspoon loose tea in for each person, 1 for the pot. Fill with hot boiling water. Cover with tea cozy or brew on top of cooker. Using tea cozy method, let tea steep the proper number of minutes,

5 for a small pot, 7 minutes for a large pot. Today most of us use tea bags. Don't feel guilty if you do, the results are excellent.

GAELIC PORRIDGE

Prepare porridge oatlets to directions, 1 cup to 3 cups cold water and pinch of salt. Cook slowly till bubbly and thick. Heat bowl with hot water and toss out. Fill with porridge. Sprinkle with raw brown sugar. Add shot of Paddy's, Jamisons, or your favorite Irish. Pour top with fresh dairy cream. Serve immediately. (Use McGanns or Flahavans progress oatlets.)

FRIED EGGS

Break the eggs (preferably free range), one at a time into a saucer, then slide them into your skillet or frying pan with a mixture of lard and butter mixed, dipping over the eggs the hot grease in spoonfuls, or turn them over, frying both sides without breaking them. They require about 3 minutes cooking. We have a lovely lady from Killmaley that spends a good deal of time with us. She always says, "John, my bullet egg please!"

Is there any dish more typically Irish than bacon, fried or grilled, with fried egg for breakfast? Back, streaky, collar, or gammon rashers are all suitable for frying or grilling. Except for gammon, bacon is usually sliced thin. Unless bacon is very lean, no extra fat is needed for cooking it.

Fried rashers of bacon, Irish sausage links, and black and white pudding, and no fry traditional or not would be complete without a grilled half tomato. Serve all the preceding with a pot of strong tea and fresh wheeten soda bread and orange marmalade. Fit for king or queen.

FINES HERBES OMELETTE

A favorite of many of our guests for evening tea! Parsley, thyme, and sweet marjoram mixed makes the famous omelette aux fines herbes so popular at every wayside eatery and so popular in every corner of sunny France. Just mix herbes with eggs and cream. Fold into skillet till done.

18

OMELETTE JARDINERE

Use 2 tablespoonfuls of mixed parsley, onion, chives, shallots, and a few leaves each of sorrel and chervil, minced fine and stirred into beaten eggs before cooking. This will take a little more butter to fry than a plain omelette.

BAKED OMELET

Beat the whites and yolks of 4 or 6 eggs separately; add to the yolks a small cup of milk, a tablespoon of flour or cornstarch, a teaspoonful of baking powder, ½ teaspoonful of salt, and lastly, the stiff beaten egg whites. Bake in a well buttered pie tin about half an hour in oven. Serve the moment it's taken from oven or it may fall.

APPLE OMELET

The Apple Omelet, to be served with pork roast, is very delicate. Take 9 large tart apples (Granny Smith) or greenies, 4 eggs, 1 cup sugar, 1 tablespoonful of butter; add cinnamon or other spices of choice. Stew the apples till they are very soft; mash them so that there will be no lumps. Add butter and sugar while they are still warm, but let them cool before putting in the beaten eggs; bake this till it is brown. You may put it all in a shallow pudding dish or in 2 tin plates to bake. (It's very good.)

TOAST DISHES

French toast: Made with either day old stale bread or thick slices of French bread, or for a special treat Irish Wheeten Soda Bread. Start by breaking a few farm fresh eggs into a bowl. I use usually 1 egg per person. Add to this ½ cup whole milk per person, a teaspoonful of sugar per person, cinnamon and nutmeg to taste, and a splash of vanilla. Beat well. Dip slices and coat well. Put onto griddle and fry on both sides. Serve with syrup, jam, or a dusting of confectioners sugar powder. Preceding excellent with fried rashers.

NUNS TOAST

Cut 4 or 5 hard-boiled eggs (farm fresh) into slices. Put a piece of butter half the size of an egg into a saucepan. When it begins to bubble, add a finely chopped onion. Let the onion cook a little without letting it take color, then stir in a teaspoonful of flour. Continue to cook. Add a cupful of milk and stir until it is smooth, then add the slices of egg and let them get hot. Pour over neatly trimmed slices of toast, hot and buttered, a tad of salt and pepper added to sauce before serving, chopped parsley for color and garnish.

CHEESE TOAST

Pour a half ounce of melted butter into frying pan. When hot, add gradually 4 ounces of mild Cheddar cheese. Whisk thoroughly until melted. Beat together half a pint of cream and 2 eggs; whisk into the cheese. Add a pinch of salt. Pour over crisp toast and serve. The preceding is usually called *Welsh Rarebit*. To make a *golden buck,* add 2 slices of pan fried bacon or rasher on each serving.

MUSHROOMS ON TOAST OR MUSHROOMS IN MADEIRA CREAM

Peel a quart of mushrooms, removing the bottom of the stem. Saute in a few tablespoons of butter. When almost done, remove to hot platter. Add flour to butter mixture and stir until smooth. Add sherry or Madeira wine, a pinch of salt and pepper, and some rich milk or cream, enough to thin. Let thicken. Add mushrooms for a few more minutes. Serve over toast with ¼ points around edges. Use lots of chopped fresh parsley for garnish.

Soups, Salads, Sauces, and Sandwiches

A HANDY SPICE AND HERB GUIDE

ALLSPICE-a pea-sized fruit that grows in Mexico, Jamaica, Central and South America. Its delicate flavor resembles a blend of cloves, cinnamon, and nutmeg. USES: (Whole) Pickles, meats, boiled fish, gravies; (Ground) Puddings, relishes, fruit preserves, baking.

BASIL-the dried leaves and stems of an herb grown in the United States and North Mediterranean area. Has an aromatic, leafy flavor. USES: For flavoring tomato dishes and tomato paste, turtle soup; also use in cooked peas, squash, snap beans; sprinkle chopped over lamb chops and poultry.

BAY LEAVES-the dried leaves of an evergreen grown in the eastern Mediterranean countries. Has a sweet, herbaceous floral spice note. USES: For pickling, stews, for spicing sauces and soup. Also use with a variety of meats and fish.

CARAWAY-the seed of a plant grown in the Netherlands. Flavor that combines the tastes of anise and dill. USES: For the cordial Kummel, baking breads; often added to sauerkraut, noodles, cheese spreads. Also adds zest to French fried potatoes, liver, canned asparagus.

CURRY POWDER-a ground blend of ginger, turmeric, fenugreek seed, as many as 16 to 20 spices. USES: For all Indian curry recipes such as lamb, chicken, and rice, eggs, vegetables, and curry puffs.

DILL-the small, dark seed of the dill plant grown in India, having a clean, aromatic taste. USES: Dill is a predominant seasoning in pickling recipes; also adds pleasing flavor to sauerkraut, potato salad, cooked macaroni, and green apple pie.

MACE-the dried covering around the nutmeg seed. Its flavor is similar to nutmeg, but with a fragrant, delicate difference. USES: (Whole) For pickling, fish, fish sauce, stewed fruit. (Ground) Delicious in baked goods, pastries, and doughnuts, adds unusual flavor to chocolate desserts.

MARJORAM-an herb of the mint family, grown in France and Chile. Has a minty-sweet flavor. USES: In beverages, jellies, and to flavor soups, stews, fish, sauces. Also excellent to sprinkle on lamb while roasting.

MSG (MONOSODIUM GLUTAMATE)-a vegetable protein derivative for raising the effectiveness of natural food flavors. USES: Small amounts, adjusted to individual taste, can be added to steaks, roasts, chops, seafoods, stews, soups, chowder, chop suey, and cooked vegetables.

OREGANO-a plant of the mint family and a species of marjoram of which the dried leaves are used to make an herb seasoning. USES: An excellent flavoring for any tomato dish, especially pizza, chili con carne, and Italian specialties.

PAPRIKA-a mild, sweet red pepper growing in Spain, Central Europe, and the United States. Slightly aromatic and prized for brilliant red color. USES: A colorful garnish for pale foods, and for seasoning Chicken Paprika, Hungarian Goulash, salad dressings.

POPPY-the seed of a flower grown in Holland. Has a rich fragrance and crunchy, nut-like flavor. USES: Excellent as a topping for breads, rolls, and cookies. Also delicious in buttered noodles.

ROSEMARY-an herb (like a curved pine needle) grown in France, Spain, and Portugal, and having a sweet fresh taste. USES: In lamb dishes, in soups, stews, and to sprinkle on beef before roasting.

SAGE-the leaf of a shrub grown in Greece, Yugoslavia, and Albania. Flavor is camphoraceous and minty. USES: For meat and poultry stuffing, sausages, meat loaf, hamburgers, stews, and salads.

THYME-the leaves and stems of a shrub grown in France and Spain. Has a strong, distinctive flavor. USES: For poultry seasoning, croquettes, fricassees, and fish dishes. Also tasty on fresh sliced tomatoes.

TURMERIC-a root of the ginger family, grown in India, Haiti, Jamaica, and Peru, having a mild, ginger-pepper flavor. USES: As a flavoring and coloring in prepared mustard and in combination with mustard as a flavoring for meats, dressings, salads.

SOUPS, SALADS, SAUCES, AND SANDWICHES

CHEF JOHN'S QUICK AND EASY VEGETABLE SOUP

1 lb. hamburger or mincemeat
1 large onion, chopped
2 stalks celery, chopped
2 qt. water
5 to 6 beef bouillon cubes

1 (15 oz.) can Veg-All
1 (15 oz.) can peeled tomatoes
½ c. Orgo's small macaroni
½ c. sliced mushrooms

Brown hamburger, onion, and celery. Add the water and bouillon cubes and let simmer about 15 minutes. Add Veg-All. Mash and add the can of tomatoes and let simmer another 15 minutes. Add macaroni and let cook another 15 minutes. Add mushrooms and simmer 5 more minutes. Serve fresh. Chopped parsley adds color and flavor at serving time.

IRISH LAMB PEA SOUP

2½ qt. water
½ c. chopped celery
¼ c. diced carrots
½ tsp. bouquet garni sachet
¼ tsp. pepper

¼ tsp. whole allspice
2 tsp. salt
1 lb. split green peas
1 lb. lamb neck slices with bone
1 medium onion, chopped

Wash peas. Drain and cook lamb pieces in kettle until some fat is rendered. Add onion and cook 5 minutes. Add water, peas, celery, carrots, and seasoning. Cover and cook over low heat 2½ to 3 hours. Remove meat. Press vegetable and liquid through sieve and return to hot plate to keep warm.

CAPE COD FISH CHOWDER

2 lb. haddock, cod, or other white
   fish
2 oz. salt pork, diced, or 2 Tbsp.
   shortening
2 onions, sliced thin
1 c. chopped celery

4 large potatoes, diced
1 large bay leaf
1 qt. milk
2 Tbsp. butter or margarine
1 tsp. salt
Freshly ground pepper to taste

Simmer white fish in 2 cups of water for 15 minutes. Drain the reserved broth and save. Remove bones from fish. Saute diced pork until crisp. Remove and set aside. Saute onions in pork fat or shortening until golden brown. Add fish, potatoes, celery, bay leaf, salt, and pepper. Pour fish broth plus enough water to make 3 cups liquid into pot and simmer 30 minutes. Add milk and butter. Simmer an additional 5 minutes. Add pepper and fresh chopped parsley if desired. Serves 8.

HAM HOCK PEA SOUP

1 lb. split green peas
1 or 2 ham hocks or seasoning of
   your choice
2 qt. water
1 large onion
1 tsp. thyme

Pepper to taste
2 or more carrots, scraped and
   diced
2 cloves garlic
2 bay leaves

Wash peas and ham hocks. Combine with rest of ingredients. Bring to a boil. Cover the pot; reduce heat and cook for 2 hours, stirring occasionally. Remove ham hocks, garlic, and bay leaves. Puree the soup through a sieve or food processor. Return to the pot and, if necessary, dilute with water.

VEGETABLE BEEF SOUP

1 lb. soup meat
5 qt. water
1 bunch celery, diced
2 large onions, diced
2 large carrots, diced
4 large potatoes, peeled and diced

1 pkg. frozen mixed vegetables
1 (16 oz.) can tomatoes, mashed
2 tsp. salt
1 tsp. pepper
1 c. uncooked rice or macaroni

Simmer soup meat in water for 2 hours in a large covered pan. Add celery, onions, carrots, potatoes, frozen vegetables, and seasonings. Let this simmer for at least 1 hour. Add macaroni or rice and cook for 30 more minutes. Test to see if seasonings meet taste. This should make 5 quarts and yield 12 seasonings. Also freezes well.

LENTIL SOUP

1 leftover ham bone or 1 slice cured
    ham (½ inch thick)
1 lb. lentils
1 green pepper
3 carrots
2 stalks celery
2 onions
1 clove garlic, crushed

Pinch of thyme
Salt and pepper to taste
3 or 4 drops of Tabasco pepper
    sauce
1 (15 oz.) can tomatoes, coarsely
    chopped
2½ qt. water

Wash and drain lentils and put in a large pot. Coarsely chop the vegetables, carrots, green pepper, celery, and onions and saute in 3 tablespoons of butter or vegetable oil. Add to the lentils with the seasonings, the water and tomatoes. Add the ham bone to pot, or if using a slice of cured ham, fry the slice a little and add to the pot. Simmer 5 or 6 hours. Add 1 teaspoon Worcestershire sauce.

CABBAGE SOUP

1 lb. stew meat, cut into 1 inch
    cubes
1 lb. lean rashers or spicy sausage
    (no casings)
1 lb. outer, dark green cabbage
    leaves
1 small, round, solid cabbage

6 diced potatoes
1 (16 oz.) can red kidney beans
2 stalks celery
4 carrots
2 medium onions, chopped
1 (16 oz.) can crushed tomatoes
Salt and pepper to taste

In a medium-size pot, put meat, rashers or sausage, potatoes, onion, and salt and pepper. Saute, then cover with water and cook over medium heat, adding celery, cabbage leaves chopped fine, cabbage, tomato, and kidney beans. Continue cooking until meat is tender and everything is cooked. Serve with crusty rolls or bread.

PARSNIP CHOWDER

¼ lb. salt pork, diced
3 onions, sliced thin
3 potatoes, sliced as thin as a 50p
   coin
2 c. parsnips, peeled and cubed
2 c. boil water

Pepper to taste
3 c. milk
1 c. cream
6 soda crackers, split, buttered, and
   toasted

Fry out salt pork until they are browned. Skim them out and drain on paper towel. Cook onions in the fat until they are transparent. Skim them out. Put in a kettle a layer of potatoes, onion, and parsnips. Repeat until kettle is well filled. Pour boiling water over vegetables and cook until soft, 20 to 30 minutes. Add pepper from the grinder. Scald the milk and cream and add to the kettle. Bring the mixture just to a boil. Take kettle off fire. Scatter in the salt pork cracklings. Serve the crackers separately to be broken into chowder or eaten as is.

IRISH POTATO SOUP

Peel and boil 8 medium size potatoes with a large onion (sliced), some herbs, and salt and pepper. Press all through a colander, then thin it with rich milk or light cream. Add a lump of butter and more seasoning if necessary. Let it heat well and serve hot.

My grandfather and others of the time would have eaten this 3 times a day. Born in Co.-Clare and brought up on tales of the terrible potato famine of 1845, they prized the King Potato above all other foods.

GALWAY BAY OYSTER STEW

   For 6:

2 c. milk
2 c. cream
1 tsp. salt
¼ tsp. pepper

Pinch of paprika (optional)
Pinch of nutmeg (optional)
4 Tbsp. butter
1 qt. oysters

Two pans needed. In one, heat milk and cream with seasonings. In the other, melt the butter. When it starts to froth, put in oysters and cook till the edges curl. The milk and cream should be scalded, not boiling. Combine. Serve at once in hot soup bowls with buttered crackers.

COCK A LEEKIE SOUP

Prep time: Approximately 25 minutes. Cooking time: 2 to 2¼ hours. Serves 6 persons.

1 boiling fowl
2 lb. knuckle of veal or beef
5 to 6 pt. (U.S. 12½ to 15 c.) cold
   water to cover meat well
1 tsp. salt
¼ tsp. pepper

4 leeks
1 large whole carrot
1 whole turnip
Bunch of herbs
2 cloves
2 oz. rice

Have the fowl trussed for boiling and the veal chopped into 3 pieces. Wipe fowl with a cloth wrung out in hot water; wash knuckle. Put into large saucepan with water, salt, and pepper. Boil up and skim well. Add leeks (washed and cut up), carrot, turnip, herbs, and cloves. Simmer 1½ hours. Wash the rice. Add to the soup; simmer another 20 minutes or until tender, skimming during boiling. Remove carrot, turnip, and herbs. Take up chicken and veal knuckle. Cut the chicken in half. Reserve ½ to be eaten cold or any other way. Cut the meat from the remaining half in neat pieces and return to soup. Reboil soup and pour into tureen.

NAVY BEAN AND BACON SOUP

1 lb. white, small navy beans,
   soaked overnight
2 small medium onions, chopped
2 large cans tomatoes, crushed

1 bay leaf
1 Tbsp. dried parsley
½ lb. rashers (lean), chopped

In medium stockpot, put 3 quarts water with washed beans that were soaked overnight. Add lean chopped rashers, bay, parsley, onions, and canned tomatoes and bring to rapid boil, then let simmer for 2 to 3 hours until beans are done and soup thickens.

CORREGEON SEAWEED FISH CHOWDER

2 c. milk with a fistful of corregeon,
   prewashed and cooked slowly
1 pt. fish stock
½ c. scallops
½ c. turbot

½ c. sole
½ c. salmon
Prawns, lobster, potatoes, mussels,
   and clams

Saute bacon and onion to taste. Add fish stock. Cook slowly, then add scallops, turbot, sole, and salmon. Last, add prawns, lobster, and potatoes. Just before serving add the precooked corregeon, mussels, clams, and a fistful of chopped corregeon. Garnish with parsley and dill.

TURNIP AND BACON SOUP

1 c. streaky bacon (rather fat)
1 c. chopped onions
1 c. chopped potatoes
3 c. chopped Swede turnips

6 c. stock
Salt and pepper to taste
1 Tbsp. chopped parsley

Saute onions with chopped bacon. Add potatoes, turnips (diced), stock, salt and pepper, and parsley. Cook 1 hour or until turnips are tender and soup ready. Serves 6 to 8.

NICOISE SALAD

½ c. salad oil
2 Tbsp. vinegar
2 Tbsp. lemon juice
2 tsp. sugar
1 tsp. paprika
1 tsp. prepared mustard
½ tsp. salt
1 medium size head lettuce, torn
    into bite-size pieces
1 (16 oz.) can whole or cut green
    beans, drained

2 c. peeled, diced, and cooked
    potatoes
1 (6½ or 7 oz.) can tuna, drained
    and broken up
2 medium tomatoes, peeled and
    sliced
2 eggs, hard-boiled and cut into
    wedges

In screw-top jar, combine salad oil, vinegar, lemon juice, sugar, paprika, prepared mustard, and salt. Cover and shake until thoroughly blended and chill. Just before serving, arrange lettuce on plate. Shake dressing and drizzle some on lettuce. Arrange beans, potatoes, tuna, and tomatoes atop lettuce. Garnish with egg wedges. Season with salt and pepper and pour more dressing over salad. Serves 6.

MARINATED VEGETABLE SALAD

1 can tiny, whole green beans
1 can baby carrots
1 can small, whole beets

1 can tiny boiled onions
1 bottle oil and vinegar dressing

Drain and marinate all the vegetables for several hours. Serve on crisp lettuce. Serves 8 to 10.

COPPER PENNY SALAD

2 bunches carrots
1 green pepper, chopped
1 medium onion, chopped
1 can tomato soup (undiluted)
½ c. salad oil

1 c. sugar
¾ c. vinegar
1 tsp. prepared mustard
1 tsp. Worcestershire sauce

Clean and slice carrots crosswise and cook until tender. Drain. Mix the remaining ingredients and cook. Add to drained carrots. Serve cold. Serves 6 to 8.

TANGY CAULIFLOWER SALAD

1 medium head cauliflower,
    separated into flowerettes
½ c. French dressing
3 shredded carrots

½ c. sliced, stuffed olives
½ c. crumbled Blue cheese
Lettuce

Parboil cauliflower so still firm. Drain. Toss with carrots, olives, and Blue cheese. Arrange on lettuce and pour dressing over. Serves 6.

SCALLOPED OYSTERS

Use a shallow baking dish. For best results, cook only 2 layers of oysters as the bottom ones will be toughened by overcooking.

1 c. soda cracker crumbs
2 c. bread, buttered and cut into
    small cubes or croutons
2 Tbsp. thick cream
2 Tbsp. sherry
¼ c. oyster liquor, strained

¼ c. melted butter
½ tsp. salt
¼ tsp. pepper
¼ tsp. nutmeg
1 qt. oysters
¼ c. butter (extra)

Roll crackers into fine crumbs. Butter bread and cut into small cubes. Mix with cracker crumbs. Mix cream, sherry, oyster liquid, melted butter, and seasonings. Mix with bread crumb mixture. This should not be too wet as the oysters supply moisture. Add more crumbs if necessary. Butter your dish. Cover the bottom with a thin layer of crumbs. Add half the oysters. Cover with more crumbs. Add the rest of the oysters. Top with the rest of the crumbs. Dot with the extra butter. Bake for 10 minutes at 450°. Reduce heat to 400° and bake till the top is well browned, 15 to 20 minutes longer.

POPPY SEED DRESSING

To be served with a grapefruit salad on lettuce or with orange segments and red onion on lettuce.

¾ c. sugar
1 tsp. dry mustard
1 tsp. poppy seeds
1 tsp. salt

⅓ c. cider vinegar
1½ Tbsp. fresh onion juice (see
    note)
1 c. corn oil

In a small bowl with electric beater at low speed, mix together sugar, mustard, poppy seeds, and salt. Add vinegar and onion juice. With beater at medium speed, beat for 3 minutes. Gradually beat in oil in thin, steady stream until thick. Store in a tightly covered jar in the refrigerator. Makes 1 pint.

Note: To make onion juice, cut a small onion in half, leaving the skin on. Using a hand juicer, extract the juice and onion pulp.

CHICKEN CHUTNEY SALAD

2 c. diced, cooked chicken
1 (13 oz.) can pineapple tidbits,
    drained
1 c. chopped celery
½ c. sliced spring onions or
    scallions
¼ c. salted peanuts

⅔ c. mayonnaise
2 Tbsp. chutney, chopped
½ tsp. lemon or lime rind
2 Tbsp. fresh lemon or lime juice
½ tsp. curry powder
¼ tsp. salt

Combine mayonnaise and rest of ingredients. Add to chicken mixture. (You may want to add more curry powder.)

CURRY POPPY SEED DRESSING

½ c. sugar
½ c. honey
1 tsp. grated onion
1 tsp. dry mustard
¼ tsp. salt
1 tsp. curry powder

6 Tbsp. tarragon vinegar
3 Tbsp. lemon juice
1 c. salad oil
1 tsp. paprika
2 tsp. poppy seeds

Put all ingredients in a jar and shake thoroughly. Serve over chopped fresh fruits mixed with thawed frozen coconut. Serve on lettuce.

MAKE-AHEAD BEAN SALAD

1 can green beans
1 can wax yellow beans
1 can chickpeas
1 can small kidney beans

6 to 8 oz. Italian dressing
1 can pitted black olives
1 jar pimentos, diced
1 onion, sliced (preferably red)

Drain beans, peas, olives, and pimentos. Put all together in large bowl that has a cover. Salt and pepper to taste. Add onion rings and dressing. Cover and refrigerate. This salad keeps and tastes better a couple of days old.

MONTE CRISTO SANDWICH AU GRATIN

6 slices bread
1 c. shredded Cheddar cheese
Turkey and ham slices
3 eggs, slightly beaten
3 Tbsp. water

2 Tbsp. corn oil
½ c. milk
½ c. mayonnaise
⅛ tsp. garlic and nutmeg

Make sandwich with turkey or ham or both. Beat eggs with water. Dip sandwiches in egg mixture. Fry both sides in corn oil until golden brown. Place in baking dish. Mix remaining ingredients in small saucepan. Heat, stirring constantly, until mixture thickens and cheese melts. Pour over toasted sandwiches and broil 3 to 5 minutes or until bubbly. Serves 3.

Notes

Main Dishes

MEAT ROASTING GUIDE

Cut	Weight Pounds	Approx. Time (Hours) (325° oven)	Internal Temperature
BEEF			
Standing rib roast			
(10 inch) ribs	4	1¾	140° (rare)
(If using shorter cut (8-inch)		2	160° (medium)
ribs, allow 30 min. longer)		2½	170° (well done)
	8	2½	140° (rare)
		3	160° (medium)
		4½	170° (well done)
Rolled ribs	4	2	140° (rare)
		2½	160° (medium)
		3	170° (well done)
	6	3	140° (rare)
		3¼	160° (medium)
		4	170° (well done)
Rolled rump	5	2¼	140° (rare)
(Roast only if high quality.		3	160° (medium)
Otherwise, braise.)		3¼	170° (well done)
Sirloin tip	3	1½	140° (rare)
(Roast only if high quality.		2	160° (medium)
Otherwise, braise.)		2¼	170° (well done)
LAMB			
Leg	6	3	175° (medium)
		3½	180° (well done)
	8	4	175° (medium)
		4½	180° (well done)
VEAL			
Leg (piece)	5	2½ to 3	170° (well done)
Shoulder	6	3½	170° (well done)
Rolled shoulder	3 to 5	3 to 3½	170° (well done)

POULTRY ROASTING GUIDE

Type of Poultry	Ready-To-Cook Weight	Oven Temperature	Approx. Total Roasting Time
TURKEY	6 to 8 lb.	325°	2½ to 3 hr.
	8 to 12 lb.	325°	3 to 3½ hr.
	12 to 16 lb.	325°	3½ to 4 hr.
	16 to 20 lb.	325°	4 to 4½ hr.
	20 to 24 lb.	300°	5 to 6 hr.
CHICKEN	2 to 2½ lb.	400°	1 to 1½ hr.
(Unstuffed)	2½ to 4 lb.	400°	1½ to 2½ hr.
	4 to 8 lb.	325°	3 to 5 hr.
DUCK	3 to 5 lb.	325°	2½ to 3 hr.
(Unstuffed)			

NOTE: Small chickens are roasted at 400° so that they brown well in the short cooking time. They may also be done at 325° but will take longer and will not be as brown. Increase cooking time 15 to 20 minutes for stuffed chicken and duck.

MAIN DISHES

ROAST PORK WITH SINFUL STUFFING

Holiday fare or for special occasion.

1 c. pitted prunes, halved
½ c. dried apricots, halved
1 c. Irish whiskey
1 tsp. grated lemon rind and 1 tsp. orange rind
1 apple, peeled and cut into ½ inch chunks
1 Tbsp. honey

1 (5 to 6 lb.) pork roast, boned and butterflied (opened)
Salt and pepper
1 clove of garlic
4 Tbsp. sweet butter, softened
1 Tbsp. dried thyme
2 Tbsp. flour
1 c. apple cider

Soak prunes and apricots in whiskey 2 or 3 hours. Add both rinds, chopped apple, and honey. Mix gently. Reserve extra liquor. Preheat oven to 325°. Open butterflied roast. Sprinkle with salt and pepper. Lay boozy fruit in strip away from both ends to prevent falling out. Tie with butcher twine. Cut slits. Insert garlic slices. Rub roast with soft butter. Sprinkle with thyme and flour. Roast on rack in roasting pan. Add cider and extra liquor. Roast 25 minutes per pound. Baste frequently. Cover with foil. Serves 6 to 8.

POTTED MEAT

½ lb. cooked leftover meat
2 oz. bacon or ham
Salt and pepper
1 tsp. mixed spice

1 tsp. prepared mustard
2 oz. butter (½ added to meat mixture)

Mince the meat and bacon or ham. Add spices. Pack into small casserole or ramekin. Seal with butter on top. Refrigerate overnight. Serve with crackers for starters.

MARINADE FOR LEG OF LAMB, PORK ROAST, OR LONDON BROIL FLANK STEAK

1 c. beer
¼ c. soy sauce
½ tsp. Worcestershire sauce
1 Tbsp. dry mustard
1 tsp. ground ginger

6 Tbsp. orange marmalade
3 cloves pressed garlic
½ tsp. salt
¼ tsp. pepper

Combine all ingredients and marinate meat overnight in covered casserole.

CITRUS LAMB

1 (5 to 6 lb.) leg of lamb
Salt
Pepper
Paprika
Juice of 1 lemon or jar juice
1 c. water

3 Tbsp. butter
2 onions, sliced
2 stalks celery, sliced
2 Tbsp. Worcestershire sauce
½ c. chili sauce
½ c. marmalade (orange)

Sprinkle lamb with salt, pepper, paprika, and lemon juice. Place onions and celery in bottom of roaster pan; add water and butter and set lamb on top of vegetables. Roast in preheated 325° oven for 30 minutes. Add Worcestershire sauce and chili sauce. (Pour over lamb.) Baste frequently, adding water if needed, and allow 30 minutes to the pound for complete roasting time. Spread marmalade over lamb for glaze and return to oven for last 30 minutes of cooking time. Serves 5 at the most.

BEEF STEW
(Hunter's style)

2½ lb. beef stew meat, cut into medium size chunks
4 or 5 onions, cut in hunks
8 carrots, cut in hunks
4 stalks celery, cut in hunks

½ c. tomato or V-8 juice
4 to 5 potatoes, cut in hunks
1 pkg. frozen green beans
3 Tbsp. Minute tapioca

Layer in casserole. Cover and bake for 4 hours in 250°F. oven. *Do not peek!*

COLLAR BACON

Prep time: 2 to 3 hours, for soaking. Cooking time: 1 hour 40 minutes.

To serve 8 persons you will need:

4 lb. cut of collar bacon
2 doz. cloves

1 tsp. mustard
4 oz. brown sugar

Soak the joint for 2 to 3 hours. Place in a pan of cold water. Bring to the boil and simmer 1 hour. Remove from pan and strip off the rind. With a sharp knife, score the fat crisscross. Decorate cloves, whole or ground, sprinkled over bacon with mustard and brown sugar made into a paste and spread over. Bake in a moderate hot oven, 400°F., or gas mark 6 for 40 minutes, basting occasionally with sauce. Garnish with parsley sprigs and serve with buttered potatoes and peas. Marrow fat peas are the best.

BOILED BACON

Prep time: 10 to 15 minutes. Cooking time: 2 to 2¼ hours.

4 lb. boned rolled forehock bacon
1 bay leaf

6 peppercorns

Soak bacon 2 hours if unsmoked, 4 hours if smoked. Rinse and put into a saucepan with the bay leaf and peppercorns. Just cover with cold water and bring to boil. Reduce heat and simmer for 1¼ hours. Remove joint and strip skin off. Slice and serve. Serves 8.

CALF'S LIVER AND BACON

Calf's liver is considered the tenderest and best flavored of all livers; it is certainly the most expensive. Calf's liver is classed as a dish for the epicure served as a main course. Too good to be treated as a mere breakfast dish. Fry the bacon rashers. Remove and keep warm. Dust the liver with flour and slice a few onion rings and flour also. Fry very briefly in bacon fat. Arrange on a serving dish and serve.

We use in Ireland, lamb's liver, as they do not kill young bullocks like we do in the states for the veal.

GRILLED GAMMON RASHERS
(Entree)

Prep time: 20 minutes after soaking. Cooking time: 10 to 15 minutes. Serves 4 to 5.

4 to 5 gammon rashers (½ inch thick)	1 oz. cloves
	8 oz. tomatoes
2 oz. melted butter	Parsley to garnish

Soak rashers in cold water for 30 minutes; dry them well. Remove rinds and brown edges. Make snips with scissors through the fat, about ½ inch apart. Brush 1 side of the rashers with melted butter. Brush grid in grill pan with butter, then lay on the rashers, buttered side up, and put under hot grille for 4 minutes. Turn the rashers over. Brush second side with butter and push a clove in each cut section of fat. Put back under grill for 3 to 4 minutes; lower heat and grill for 3 minutes longer.

HAMBURGER MINCE STROGANOFF

2 Tbsp. shortening	1 c. evaporated milk
1½ lb. mince	3 Tbsp. catsup
1 onion, thinly sliced	2 Tbsp. Worcestershire sauce
3 Tbsp. flour	Salt, pepper, and garlic salt to taste
1 can condensed consomme or beef cube and water	¼ c. sherry

Brown meat and onion in shortening. Sprinkle flour over meat and stir until well blended. Add consomme, milk, catsup, and Worcestershire. Cook, stirring until thickened. Add seasonings and simmer 10 minutes. Just before serving, add sherry. Serve with buttered noodles or rice. Mushrooms may be also added the last 10 minutes.

FARMYARD SAUSAGE SOUFFLE

6 slices white bread, crust removed and cut into cubes	1 tsp. dry mustard
	2 c. milk
1 lb. pork sausage, browned and drained	1 tsp. salt
	1 c. mild Cheddar cheese, shredded
8 eggs	

Grease 9x13 inch glass pan. Put layer of bread on bottom, then sausage meat. Beat eggs. Add milk, salt, and mustard; pour over bread. Top with cheese and cover with Saran Wrap. Put in fridge overnight. Bake 45 minutes at 350°F. Serves 8.

YORKSHIRE PUDDING

1½ c. flour	1½ c. water or milk
¼ tsp. baking powder	2 eggs
½ tsp. salt	

Mix dry ingredients. Add liquid gradually. Add eggs. Beat very well with beater. Let stand for half hour or more. It may need thinning after it has waited. Batter should be the consistency of almost water. Bake in roasting pan or in a metal dish, 12x12 inches or larger. Put in beef drippings from roast. Have pan and drippings very hot, 400°, then pour in batter. Bake 25 to 30 minutes at 400° oven. Serve at once with roast beef. Have plenty of hot gravy on hand.

BAKED PORK CHOPS

4 pork chops (double for 8)
Salt and pepper
Flour

1 c. uncooked Minute rice
¾ c. orange juice
1 can mushroom soup

Flour pork chops. Salt and pepper them and brown them in skillet. One large chop per person. Put into baking dish. Sprinkle with 1 cup uncooked rice over and around chops. Pour ¾ cup orange juice over chops. Add 1 can mushroom soup. (Do not dilute.) Put over and around chops. Cover dish with foil. Bake 1½ hours at 350°F.

Variations on the recipe could be that chicken quarters may be substituted for the pork chops with equal success. Also, 1 can tomatoes (large crushed) and several onions, peeled and sliced thin could be substituted for the orange juice using the same method.

MINCE LOAF

The best I've ever had.

1 egg
1 tsp. salt (optional)
¼ tsp. pepper
1 Tbsp. brown sugar
½ tsp. dried leaf basil
½ tsp. dried leaf thyme
¼ c. ketchup
2 tsp. prepared mustard
1½ c. soft bread crumbs

2 beef bouillon cubes, dissolved in
   1 cup boiling water
½ c. finely chopped celery
½ c. finely chopped onion
1 c. shredded Cheddar or Swiss
   cheese
2 lb. ground mince beef (chuck or
   meat loaf mix)

Beat egg lightly in bowl. Add salt, pepper, basil, thyme, ketchup, mustard, bread crumbs, and bouillon. Mix well. Mix in celery, onion, and cheese. Add ground meat and mix lightly but thoroughly. Form into loaf shape on baking sheet or place in 9x5x3 inch loaf pan. Bake, uncovered, at 375°F. for 1 hour. Makes 7 to 10 servings.

SAUERBRATEN - AMERICAN STYLE

3 slices stale bread
1 lb. ground beef (mince)
1 medium onion, minced
1 egg
1½ tsp. salt
8 gingersnaps

½ lb. wide noodles, cooked
2 Tbsp. margarine
1½ c. vinegar
1½ c. water
10 whole cloves
5 bay leaves

Soak bread in a little warm water. Crumble. Add meat, onion, egg, and salt; mix well. Shape into 4 patties. Brown on both sides in margarine. Add vinegar, water, cloves, and bay leaves. Cover and simmer 1 hour. Add crumbled gingersnaps to water liquid. Blend until smooth. Serve over hot noodles. Good with braised red cabbage, beer, and dark bread.

BAKED STUFFED CABBAGE

Use large, round whole head with some loose outer leaves.

3 c. water
1 c. brown rice
1 lb. lean ground mince
1 egg
¼ c. grated onion
¼ c. grated carrot
⅓ c. grated raw potato
1½ tsp. salt

Freshly ground black pepper
1 large onion, sliced
¼ c. seedless white raisins
⅓ c. brown sugar
3 c. canned crushed tomatoes
4 Tbsp. fresh lemon juice or wine
 vinegar

1. Cook whole cabbage in a large pot of boiling water for 10 minutes. Remove cabbage from pot and detach as many outer leaves as possible without breaking them. Return the cabbage to the boiling water and cook 10 more minutes. Remove and again detach as many leaves as possible. Repeat until there are 18 leaves. Trim tough inner rib end from outer cabbage leaves.

2. Bring 3 cups water to boil. Add rice and cook 15 minutes. Drain.

3. In a large bowl, mix rice, mince beef, egg, grated onion, carrot, potato, and 1 teaspoon salt and pepper.

4. Place 2 heaping tablespoons of mixture in center of each leaf. Fold in sides and roll up tightly.

5. In bottom of a shallow 3 quart baking pan, place a layer of sliced onions. Arrange cabbage rolls on top.

6. In a medium saucepan, combine raisins, brown sugar, tomatoes, salt, and lemon juice and bring to a boil. Taste sauce. Add more salt or brown sugar if necessary.

7. Pour mixture over cabbage rolls. Cover tightly and bake in a 350°F. oven 60 to 90 minutes or until the cabbage is tender and rice is completely cooked. Makes 8 servings.

MARINATED EYE OF THE ROUND

Grill or roast these tender, flavor packed roasts. You can easily halve the recipe.

2 (2 to 2½ lb.) boneless beef eye of
 round roasts
Seasoned salt or salt
Lemon pepper seasoning
½ c. soy sauce
¼ c. Italian dressing (oil and vinegar
 for salad)

¼ c. Irish or other whiskey
¼ c. Worcestershire sauce
Grated carrot
Parsley sprigs

1. Pierce roasts in several places with a sharp knife. Season roasts lightly with seasoned salt and lemon pepper seasoning. Place roasts in a large plastic bag. Set in a deep bowl.

2. For marinade, in a small bowl, stir together soy sauce, salad dressing, whiskey, and Worcestershire sauce. Pour over roasts. Seal bag and marinate in the refrigerator overnight, turning occasionally. Remove roasts after marinating to grill. Place roasts on grill rack over drip pan out, not over, the coals. Lower grill hood. Grill roasts 1 to 1¼ hours or till the thermometer registers 140°, or roast in 325°F. oven for 1¼ to 1¾ hours, basting with leftover marinade. Slice and serve. Makes 16 to 20 portions.

BOILED BEEF TONGUE

Wash fresh tongue and just cover it with water in the pot; put in ⅛ cup salt and pepper to taste. Add more water as it evaporates so as to keep the tongue nearly covered until done. When it can be easily pierced with a fork, take it out and if wanted soon, peel off skin and set tongue away to cool. If wanted for future use, do not peel until needed.

Cold Horseradish Cream: Use fresh whipped cream. Add horseradish to taste, or Hot Horseradish Sauce. Make Cream sauce (see sauces). Add fresh prepared horseradish to taste and serve with hot tongue.

TO CURE HAMS AND BACON

We had a wonderful experience back in the early 70's in Warwick, Rhode Island, at our first restaurant, a diner. A local construction worker, cum farmer, approached us to save all the garbage from the 350 meals served each day. After a year or so, I convinced him to purchase a piglet for ourselves. It was garbage fed till just before slaughter.

To cure hams and bacon: For each 100 pounds of hams, make a pickle of 10 pounds of salt, 2 pounds brown sugar, 2 ounces saltpeter, 1 ounce of red pepper, and from 4 to 4½ gallons of water, or just enough to cover hams after being packed in a watertight vessel, or enough salt to make a brine to float a fresh egg high enough, that is to say, out of water. First rub hams with common salt and lay them into a tub. Take preceding ingredients. Put them into a vessel over the fire and heat it hot, stirring frequently. Remove any scum. Allow it to boil 10 minutes; let it cool and pour over meat after laying in brine 5 or 6 weeks. Take out. Drain and wipe and smoke from 2 to 3 weeks. Small bacon, 2 weeks in pickle is enough.

CELTIC CUISINE
Baked Limerick Ham. (From County Limerick, Ireland.)

1 ham	½ lb. brown sugar
½ glass brandy	4 oz. butter
½ pt. beer	¼ oz. cloves

1. Bake ham for 4½ hours in oven at 300°.
2. When cooked, remove skin and make a paste with the brandy, butter, and sugar.
3. Coat ham with the paste and stick in the cloves.
4. Bake in oven until a nice golden brown.
5. Pour beer over ham. Serve hot or cold.

IRISH LAMB STEW

2½ lb. boneless shoulder or leg of lamb, cut into 1 inch cubes	¼ tsp. parsley
2½ c. water	3 medium potatoes, halved
2 tsp. salt	6 small onions
2 Tbsp. butter	¼ lb. mushrooms, halved
¼ tsp. pepper	1 c. half & half or milk
¼ tsp. thyme	¼ c. flour
	1½ lb. fresh or frozen peas

Brown lamb cubes in butter in large Dutch oven or kettle. Add water and seasonings; cover. Simmer 20 minutes. Add potatoes and onions; simmer, covered, 15 minutes. Add peas and mushrooms. Simmer, covered, 15 minutes or until lamb and vegetables are tender. Blend half & half with flour. Stir into bubbling stew and boil 2 or 3 more minutes, stirring constantly. Correct seasonings if necessary and serve.

GRILLED GIGOT CHOPS

Prep time: 15 minutes, including sauce. Cooking time: 20 minutes.

To serve 4 you will need:

4 gigot chops (lamb, cut from the leg)	½ pt. (U.S. 1¼ c.) water
Salt and pepper	½ oz. butter
2 Tbsp. cooking oil	1 Tbsp. sugar
Parsley	Grated rind ½ lemon
8 oz. green gooseberries	Pinch of mixed cake spice
	1 tsp. chopped mint

Prepare and if necessary, trim the chops. Brush the bars of the grill pan with oil and heat grill. Brush chops over with oil, then season with salt and pepper. Place chops under hot grill, turning them over after 2 to 3 minutes to grill other side. Reduce heat and continue cooking about 15 minutes, turning the chops from time to time. Arrange the chops on platter. Garnish with parsley. Serve with Gooseberry Sauce.

Sauce: Top and tail gooseberries; stew in water until soft. Beat well, then run through nylon sieve. Return to pan. Beat in butter and sugar and reheat. Add lemon rind, spice, and mint.

STEWED BEEF KIDNEY

Cut the kidney into slices. Season highly with salt and pepper. Fry it a light brown. Take out slices, then pour a little warm water into the pan. Dredge in same flour. Put slices of kidney in again. Let them stew very gently; add some parsley. Sheep's kidneys may be split open, broiled under gas flame, and served with a piece of butter placed on each half.

Notes

Holiday Fare -

Game Suppers

GRILLING TIPS

1. To clean the grilling surface, heat grill for five minutes, then brush with a wire brush to loosen debris.
2. When cooking meats without sauce, oil the grill with one to two tablespoons of vegetable or olive oil to prevent meat from sticking.
3. Trim cuts of meat of all excess fat before grilling, leaving ¼ inch around the edges.
4. Ribs will cook better when simmered for approximately one hour in water before grilling. This process removes fat from the ribs, and will prevent flare-ups on the grill.
5. Cuts of beef and lamb for outdoor grilling should be a minimum of 1½ inches thick, but not more than three inches thick, to retain pink inside after the surface sears.
6. When marinating small cuts of meat, allow three hours per inch of thickness in refrigerator. For larger cuts of meat, allow one to two days in the refrigerator, depending on the size of the cut. Turn the meat occasionally to distribute the marinade.
7. Always marinate in a noncorrosive container, such as glass, porcelain, glazed earthenware or stainless steel.
8. Use tongs to turn meat and fish. Piercing the food will let the juices escape.
9. When using bamboo skewers for kabobs, soak them in water for at least 30 minutes before use to prevent them from burning.
10. Cutting into meat to check for doneness will let the juices escape. Instead of cutting, touch the meat. If it is firm to the touch, then it is well done. If it feels very soft, it is still raw. If it feels soft to the touch but springs back, it is medium rare. (Be careful not to burn yourself.)
11. Chicken with bones can be baked in an oven for 15 to 20 minutes, covered, at 300° before grilling. Alternatively, parboil for about five minutes (with or without skin). This keeps grilling time down and prevents chicken from drying out.
12. Remove skin, clean and parboil chicken. Cover with barbecue sauce or other marinade and freeze in an appropriate quantity for your meal. This gets the mess and work behind you and allows the marinade to be absorbed. Thaw when you are ready to grill.
13. Chicken cutlets can be grilled quickly over high heat. Do not overcook! Use a grilling basket if pieces are small.
14. To test chicken for doneness, light meat should be white and the juice translucent, not pink; dark meat juices should be clear.
15. It is difficult to keep fish from sticking to the grill. Thicker cuts and fish steaks work best. The easiest solution is a grilling basket, sprayed with Pam.
16. Fish is done if opaque throughout. Do not overcook!
17. Hard vegetables, such as cauliflower, broccoli, and small onions, should be parboiled approximately 1½ minutes before putting on skewers. Soft vegetables, such as cherry tomatoes and mushrooms, can be boiled for 30-45 seconds.
18. One inch cross sections of corn on the cob make a nice addition to kabobs.
19. Marinate sliced eggplant or zucchini in Italian dressing overnight then grill as desired.
20. Do not mix items on a kabob that require different cooking times, such as steak and mushrooms. Segregate items on separate skewers to adjust times. It is not as pretty, but it avoids a cooking disaster.
21. Be creative with marinades, but do not forget old stand-bys such a bottle of Catalina dressing for chicken or a mixture of Italian dressing (one bottle) and tomato paste (large can) for beef kabobs. All you need for fish is some tamari sauce (similar to soy sauce) and a few drops of oil.

HOLIDAY FARE - GAME SUPPERS

POULTRY AND GAME

Chicken: The hen is the oldest domestic bird in Ireland; at one time, every countrywoman and many townswomen with back gardens kept a few hens and a cockerel to supply the family with eggs and the occasional chicken for the table, selling the surplus for "pin" money, for the chicken and egg money was recognized as her "perks." Even on the farm, the chickens and eggs were the special care of the farmer's wife.

Most birds are killed while young; this means that although they are tender, they are not as tasty as older birds. Oven ready birds can be bought from the grocer, butcher, or supermarket, as well as the poulterers. If you have time to shop around, free range chickens are better for flavor. It helps to know the type of bird to ask for. Thus, baby chickens (poussins) weighing from ¾ to 1½ pounds can be split in halves and are most delicious for grilling or barbeque. The flesh is so tender that they are cooked in no time at all.

Spring chickens come next. Known as poulets, and they are usually cut into 4 or 6 pieces for frying; they weigh from 2½ to 3½ pounds. Over that weight up to 4½ pounds, we get full grown fowls (poulards), requiring the longer process of cooking, roasting, or casseroling. Older birds over 4½ pounds are broiling fowls, but can be casseroled whole or in joints. A capon is a male chicken castrated when young to increase weight quickly and improve flavor. They grow as large as old cockerels, but the flesh remains tender. They can be roasted.

DIJON CHICKEN

4 boneless chicken breasts
Dijon mustard
Lemon juice
Salt and pepper
Worcestershire sauce

Pull skin and fat off chicken breasts and brush them entirely with Dijon mustard (Grey Poupon). Fill a large bowl with ¼ cup of lemon juice and 2 teaspoons Worcestershire sauce. Put breasts in bowl and let set for at least 15 minutes or as long as overnight. Bake at 350° for 25 to 30 minutes.

ORIENTAL CHICKEN THIGHS

Skin and lightly saute thighs.

Sauce:

1 Tbsp. butter
Soy sauce
1 c. brown sugar
1 c. apple juice
¼ c. cider vinegar
Garlic
Ginger

Thicken with 2 tablespoons cornstarch with water.

Stir-fry sauce:

⅓ c. Italian dressing　　　　　　　　**1 tsp. light brown sugar**
1 Tbsp. soy sauce　　　　　　　　　　**¼ tsp. ginger**

BAKED CHICKEN IN SOUR CREAM

Pour over cut up chicken pieces (breasts are best) 1 carton sour cream, 1½ or 2 cans cream of chicken soup, ½ cup sherry, and 1 can mushrooms with liquid. Bake at 350° for 1½ hour, turning chicken once or basting.

WILD DUCKS

Most wild ducks are apt to have the flavor of fish and in the hands of inexperienced cooks are sometimes unpalatable on this account. Before roasting them, parboil them with a small peeled carrot put within each duck. This absorbs the unpleasant taste. An onion will have the same effect, but unless your using onion in the stuffing, the carrot is better. Roast the same as a tame duck or put the duck with a whole onion, peeled, plenty salt and pepper, and a glass of claret. Bake in a hot oven 20 minutes. Serve hot with gravy it yields in cooking and currant jelly on side.

Several years ago we had the pleasure of visiting a cousin and her husband in Blakney, Norfolk, England. They live near Marshland and use the reeds for thatching old English cottages. They have organized shoots for game birds and Brigid, my cousin, prepares wonderful game suppers for the guests. We spent a week over and I had the pleasure of her Aga cooker for roasting wild ducks, teal, partridge, woodcock, and quail. This means of cooking is far superior to a gas or electric cooker.

SOME TIPS FOR ROASTING THE SUNDAY TURKEY

1. Turn the turkey upside-down upon removing it from the oven. That way all the juices immediately run to the breast meat to keep it moist and tasty.
2. A variation is to baste the turkey with a garlic-herb butter. Take a couple of cloves of garlic and maybe a little shallot, then saute them in whole butter; add fresh herbs (that's critical), thyme, sage, and a stem of rosemary. It gives your turkey a beautiful golden color and wonderful flavor.
3. Cook your stuffing or dressing outside the bird in a separate pan. This cuts down on the total cooking time for the turkey and it prevents a chance of salmonella with mingling bacteria. To keep the stuffing moist, use cooked drippings from the bird to add to the stuffing just before it's cooked.
4. Cook lighter and enjoy the fresh foods coming back into season. For example, substitute a wild rice and vegetable dressing for the traditional bread dressing.
5. Do something out of the ordinary with your leftovers. A really nice risotto can be made from leftover turkey by mixing the rice with roasted eggplant, wild mushrooms, and your leftover vegetables. The turkey remains juicy and it's a change from just leftover sandwiches.

LEFTOVER TURKEY LASAGNA

3 c. diced turkey　　　　　　　　　　**8 oz. lasagne noodles, cooked**

Mix together:

2 cans mushroom soup
⅔ to 1 c. milk

½ tsp. salt
½ tsp. poultry seasoning

Beat together:

2 (3 oz.) pkg. cream cheese

1 c. cream style cottage cheese

Stir in:

⅓ c. sliced green or ripe olives
⅓ c. onion, diced

⅓ c. green pepper, diced
¼ c. parsley, chopped

Mix all ingredients together except noodles. Put noodles and turkey in layers in flat greased casserole. Cover and bake in 350°F. for 1 hour.

TURKEY TETRAZZINI

1 can celery or mushroom soup
1 can cream of chicken soup
½ c. mushrooms or toasted almonds
1 c. turkey broth or turkey gravy, thinned with milk

2 c. grated process cheese (American or Cheddar)
6 c. (12 oz.) cooked spaghetti
4 c. boned turkey, diced
½ c. grated Parmesan cheese
Dash of paprika

Blend soup and broth. Part of milk may be used. Stir in process cheese. Mix with cooked, cut up spaghetti, turkey, and mushrooms or nuts. Turn into greased shallow baking pan about 7½ x 12 inch. Sprinkle top with Parmesan cheese and paprika. Bake at 350°F. until bubbly and brown, 30 minutes. Serves 8 to 10.

ROAST GOOSE WITH ORANGE SAUCE

Tips on cooking fresh goose:

1. Remove the pouch of fat that is in the stomach of the goose and render it separately to use on mashed potatoes and for other cooking uses.

2. Rub the inside and outside of the goose with either garlic salt or crushed garlic and salt.

3. Place in roasting pan (rack is not important), breast side up, and place in a preheated 400°F. oven.

4. After 30 minutes, reduce the heat to 300° and baste bird with the fat that is in the pan.

5. Continue roasting for approximately 2 hours longer. The color brown of the skin is the accurate determining factor of when the goose is done. A meat thermometer will record 160° when the bird is thoroughly cooked. The goose is best served warm and should come out of the oven shortly before serving time. About 2 cups of goose fat is normal and should be saved in the fridge for future use.

1 goose (approx. 10 lb.)
Orange sections (mandarins will do)

Salt and pepper
Marjoram

For the sauce:

2 c. caramelized sugar
2 c. currant jelly
2 c. frozen concentrate orange juice
1 c. fresh or frozen concentrate
    orange juice

4 oranges, cut in halves
Orange zest for garnish
¼ c. orange liquor

Dress the goose. Season the cavity with salt, pepper, and marjoram. Stuff with onion and oranges and roast in 350°F. oven, turning to achieve full browning. Reduce heat to 325° once browned and continue roasting approximately 2 hours or until juices from the thigh run clear when pierced.

For the sauce: Caramelize the sugar by cooking over medium-high heat until brown and caramellike. Reduce heat to low. Add jelly, concentrated juice, fresh juice, and orange halves. Cook for 45 minutes on low heat and strain. Add orange zest for garnish and liquor.

ROAST PHEASANT

Prep time: 20 minutes. Cooking time: 50 minutes to 1 hour. Serves 4 to 5.

1 brace of pheasants, trussed as
    chickens
4 slices streaky bacon
8 oz. chuck steak

1 dessert spoon seasoned flour
Fried bread crumbs
Bread sauce
Red currant jelly

Wipe the birds with soft cloth; sprinkle inside and out with salt and pepper. Tie 2 slices of bacon over each bird. Divide the steak and put a piece into the cavity of each bird. The meat is meant to keep the birds moist and juicy; it is not eaten, but it will make excellent soup. Place birds in roasting pan. Put a little butter or bacon fat in pan and roast in hot oven, 450°F. or gas mark 7, for 45 to 50 minutes, basting from time to time. When nearly done, remove the bacon. Baste well. Dredge with seasoned flour and return to oven to get a good brown. Before serving, remove trussing strings and place birds on a bed of watercress. Serve with a good red wine, fried bread crumbs, bread sauce, and red currant jelly.

ROAST GROUSE

Prep time: 15 to 20 minutes. Cooking time: 30 minutes.

To serve 2 you will need:

1 brace young grouse, plucked and
    trussed as for chicken
Salt and pepper
2 oz. butter

4 rashers streaky bacon
Cooked livers of birds
2 slices toast
1 dessert spoon seasoned flour

Wipe the birds with a soft cloth; sprinkle inside and out with salt and pepper. Put 1 ounce butter inside each; tie 2 thin rashers of bacon over the breasts. Crush the cooked livers with a fork; season with salt and pepper. Spread this on toast; put toast in roasting pan or casserole dish and place birds on top. Put in hot oven, 425°F. or gas mark 7, and roast 20 to 30 minutes according to size of birds. They should be slightly underdone, but not rare. Baste 2 or 3 times with bacon fat and butter. Five minutes before they are done, remove the bacon. Dredge lightly with flour and put in hot oven, 425°F. or gas mark 7, to get a good crust. Serve on toast slices with bread sauce and clear gravy made from the giblets. It is not correct to serve vegetables with grouse other than chips and watercress and lettuce salad.

PARTRIDGES

For roasting, partridges should be shot the same year as bred and should not hang more than 3 or 4 days. They are roasted same as grouse, taking 30 to 35 minutes and served the same.

Notes

Fish -

How To Cook

What You Hook

RULES FOR USING HERBS

1. Use with a light hand - the aromatic oils are strong and objectionable if too much is used.

2. Blend or heat with butter, margarine, or oil to draw out and extend the flavor. Unsalted butter is best. When using herbs in French dressing, have the oil tepid.

3. Cut or chop leaves very fine. The more cut surface exposed, the more completely the aromatic oil is absorbed.

4. Dried herbs are two to four times stronger than fresh herbs, so that if you substitute dried for fresh herbs use ¼ to ½ the amount. Experimentation is the best guide.

5. The flavor of herbs is lost by extended cooking.

6. To taste the true flavor of an herb you have not used before, mix ½ teaspoon crushed herb with 1 tablespoon cream cheese or sweet butter, let stand 10-15 minutes. Taste on a cracker.

7. The beginner should err on the side of too little rather than too much. It is easy to overseason, and one flavor should never be allowed to overpower another. A person should not be able to recognize the presence of an herb or what accounts for the delicious flavor. More of an herb can be added, but it cannot be taken out.

8. Herbs are used in addition to salt and pepper.

9. For **herb butters,** 1 tablespoon of the minced fresh herb is mixed into ¼ pound softened butter or margarine. Let stand at room temperature for at least one hour, preferably more. After flavor has been absorbed into butter, it should be chilled in the refrigerator. This will keep for several days if covered tightly so it does not absorb odors from the refrigerator.

FISH - HOW TO COOK WHAT YOU HOOK

HOW TO COOK WHAT YOU HOOK

The simplest method of cooking "the frying pan," recommended for casual weekend cooks.

1. Dip cleaned fish in cold milk or water. Drain.
2. Sprinkle with salt and pepper. Dip into bread crumbs, corn meal, or flour.
3. Fry in hot fat ⅛ inch deep in skillet till brown on both sides (10 minutes).
4. Drain and serve piping hot.

J.M.

FILLETS OF PLAICE

Prep time: 20 to 25 minutes. Cooking time: 35 minutes. Serves 4.

1 large or 2 small plaice (about 2 lb.), filleted and cut into 4 fillets
2 oz. butter

Sauce of choice (lemon butter, mushroom, or parsley)

Wipe fish and place in shallow, well buttered ovenproof dish. Dot with 2 ounces butter. Cover and bake in a moderate oven, 350°F. or gas mark 4, for 20 minutes. Can be topped with seasoned bread crumbs and sprinkle of paprika for variation. I prefer just a wedge of lemon and butter drizzled over but the sauces are lovely also.

Note: Ireland and the Islands surrounding, making up the British Islands, are surrounded with seas rich with fish. The Islands are small so that no town is far inland. You can be pretty certain that all the fish you get anywhere is still fresh enough "to taste the sea." I often tell guests when here at Spanish Point if in doubt, choose fish. I have always said our fish is so so good that the simple methods are the best for cooking. There is no need to disguise its beautiful natural flavor.

MACKEREL BAKED STUFFED

Prep time: 20 to 25 minutes. Cooking time: 25 minutes. Serves 4.

1 mackerel (about 2 lb.)
Salt and pepper
½ pt. (U.S. 1¼ c.) bread crumbs
½ tsp. mixed herbs
1 tsp. chopped parsley
1 Tbsp. peeled shrimp (canned is okay)

Beaten egg or milk
Little margarine or drippings
Lemon, tomatoes, and cucumber for garnish

Wash fish well, removing the head. Make 4 deep gashes through the fish from the back. Season with salt and pepper. Mix the bread crumbs, herbs, and shrimp. Reserve a few shrimp for garnishing and moisten with beaten egg or milk. Arrange fish on baking dish and pack the stuffing in the gashes, piling it up well. Dot with margarine or drippings. Cover with greaseproof paper or foil and bake in a moderate oven, 350°F. or gas mark 4, for 20 to 25 minutes. Garnish with lemon, tomato, cucumber, and a few shrimp.

LOBSTERS

All lobsters are dull bluish or blackish green before they are boiled; the red color comes with cooking. Medium size lobsters are best for flavor and for tenderness. Two and one-half to 3 pounds is a good average weight. The flesh of the male lobster is firmer and better flavored than that of the female. The hen, however, contains the roe or "coral" which is valued for sauces and garnishing.

I think the best way to serve a lobster is boiling. Pick out a young 2¼ to 3 pound lobster. Bring water to rolling boil and drop lobster in for 12 to 15 minutes. When lobster is red, it is cooked. Twist off the large and small claws and crack them. Split the lobster down the center from the underside with a strong pointed knife. Remove the dark thread, spinal cord, from near the outer edge of the lobster and discard the stomach which lies near the head and gills.

If it is a hen lobster, take out the coral roe and use as a garnish. Ease the meat in the tail away from the shell without removing it. Mix the coral with a little salt and pepper and a squeeze of lemon juice and pile it near the head. Put the halves of lobster on a hot plate. Remove the meat from the claws. Supply lobster picks or metal skewers so diners can pick the meat for themselves. Serve with drawn butter or mayonnaise, cold.

SMOKED AND SALTED FISH

It is not surprising that in a country abounding in fish the curing and preserving of it early became an important culinary art; it is an art in which we excel today, even though we have the means of keeping fish in its natural state for quite a length of time. What was started as a means of preventing waste has been kept up because our smoked fish is delicious and justly world famous and, in fact, is an important export.

We purchase all of our smoked salmon, trout, mackerel, etc., from Peter Curtain dba Lisdoonvarna Smoke House, and his lovely Scandinavian wife. Smoked salmon is the aristocrat and is in the most demand, though smoked trout (not as expensive) are, in the opinion of many who really know, good eating. Much more delicious and superior. As for myself, I would go for the smoked trout first. All of these smoked delicacies need no further cooking.

Kippers are split, salted, smoked herrings. They can be grilled or pan fried and nothing should be added to them but a little butter and they need no longer than 5 minutes on each side. The Findon or finnam haddock, came originally from Findon in Scotland and is perhaps the favorite of all smoked fish. More commonly known as "Finny Haddie" it is unbeatable for its soft, tender flesh and delicate flavor. The cooking of Finny Haddies is quick and simple. Just wash it. Lay it in a buttered fry pan. Cover with milk and water, half and half. Put a lid on top and simmer for 8 to 10 minutes according to thickness. To serve, place on a hot plate with a little of the "gravy" poured over and a knob of butter on top.

FISH AND OYSTER PIE

Use any remains of cold fish such as haddock or cod, 2 dozen oysters, pepper and salt to taste, bread crumbs sufficient for the quantity of fish, ½ teaspoon of grated nutmeg, and 1 teaspoonful of finely chopped parsley. Clear the fish from the bones and put a layer of it in a pie dish. Sprinkle with salt and pepper, then a layer of bread crumbs, oysters, nutmeg, and chopped parsley. Repeat a second layer till the casserole is quite full. You may finish with a layer of bread crumbs and sprinkle with parsley and paprika. Dot with melted butter. Bake 30 minutes at 350°.

STEWED BEEF KIDNEY

Cut the kidney into slices. Season highly with salt and pepper. Fry it a light brown. Take out slices, then pour a little warm water into the pan. Dredge in same flour. Put slices of kidney in again. Let them stew very gently; add some parsley. Sheep's kidneys may be split open, broiled under gas flame, and served with a piece of butter placed on each half.

SALMON TROUT

Salmon trout should be called the sea trout. It is a sea fish but comes into fresh water to spawn. It is not as red as salmon and seldom grows to more than 3 pounds in weight, but is a true delicacy. All the ways of cooking salmon are suitable for cooking salmon trout, but do not boil it as you will ruin it. It is best baked whole. Garnish with lemon, parsley, cucumbers, and tomato.

TOMATO CREAM SAUCE FOR BROILED FISH, HALIBUT, ETC.

Sauce:

2 oz. butter	1 Tbsp. flour
1 small onion	Few spoonfuls milk
4 medium tomatoes, skinned	½ pt. (U.S. 1¼ c.) white wine and
1 Tbsp. chopped parsley	water or fish stock (half and
1 tsp. chives	half)
1 tsp. chopped thyme	1 tsp. lemon juice
1 tsp. chopped tarragon	1 egg yolk
Pinch of salt and white pepper	2 Tbsp. thin cream

Melt butter in saucepan. Fry chopped onion 3 minutes. Add 3 tomatoes, parsley, and other herbs. Salt and pepper. Cook gently 3 to 4 minutes or until tomatoes are soft. Stir well to break up tomatoes. Add flour blended to smooth cream with the 2 tablespoons milk. Stir over low heat until boiling. Add white wine and water or stock and lemon juice. Add remaining tomato cut into small dice. Stir well. Remove from pan and allow sauce to cool. Beat yolk into cream and then stir into tomato mixture. Do not allow to get near boiling lest it curdle on ye.

BATTER DIPPED DEEP FRIED FISH

2 c. flour	2 eggs
2 Tbsp. sugar	¼ c. oil
4 tsp. baking powder	¼ c. milk
1 tsp. salt	1¼ c. stale beer

Mix dry ingredients together. Beat eggs; add oil, milk, and beer. Stir until smooth. Add dry ingredients and mix well. Dry fish and dip in batter. Deep-fry until golden brown. Serve with lemon wedges and tartar sauce.

SALMON STEAKS

4 salmon steaks	Water in saucepan to cover fish
2 slices lemon (wedges, ¼ lemon)	steaks
Few slices celery and carrot	

Cook over medium heat for approximately 10 minutes until filets feel firm and when cut are not transparent.

Sauce: Use melted butter and lemon wedge. Sprinkle with dill or parsley.

HERB CRUSTED ORANGE ROUGHY

Orange roughy is that wonderful deep water fish from New Zealand. It flash freezes without loosing any of its taste or texture and it's cooked with orange juice and a crust of herbs and orange "zest."

¼ c. fresh orange juice or frozen	1 Tbsp. dried tarragon
4 fillets orange roughy or other fleshy fish	1 Tbsp. coarsely ground black pepper
Safflower oil or olive oil	Grated zest (rind) of 2 oranges

1. Preheat oven to 325°F.
2. Pour orange juice into shallow baking dish long enough to hold fish.
3. Brush fish lightly with oil; place in baking dish.
4. In a bowl, combine tarragon, pepper, and grated orange zest. Sprinkle mixture on top of fish, patting it lightly to form a thin crust.
5. Bake for 20 to 25 minutes until fish flakes easily when tested with a fork.
6. With a long metal spatula, remove fish carefully to a serving dish. Fish may release a lot of liquid while cooking. This can be discarded. Serve immediately. Serves 4.

SEAFOOD FLORENTINE PIE

1 (16 oz.) pkg. Ronzoni spaghetti or any other brand
½ c. grated Parmesan cheese
¼ c. butter or margarine
4 eggs, beaten
2 (10 oz.) pkg. frozen chopped spinach, thawed and well drained
2 eggs, beaten

2 c. cottage cheese
2 medium onions, finely chopped
2 tsp. Dijon style mustard
1 tsp. dill weed
1 c. shredded Swiss cheese
¾ lb. medium shrimp, cleaned and split
½ lb. Bay scallops

Cook pasta as directed on package. Drain. Add the Parmesan cheese, butter, and 4 eggs. Spread over bottom and sides of well greased 13x9 inch pan. Combine remaining ingredients. Spoon into pasta lined pan. Bake at 375°F. for 45 minutes. Makes 8 servings.

BAKED COD IN CREAM

Allow 1 chunk of fish per person:

1 tsp. onion for each serving
½ tsp. butter
½ c. creamy milk

1 small bay leaf
Salt and pepper

Casserole fish. Cover with milk, butter, onion, bay leaf, and salt and pepper. Cover and steam on top of stove, covered. When cooked 30 minutes, roux may be added to thicken gravy.

FRIED TROUT IN BUTTER

Prep time: 20 minutes. Cooking time: 10 to 15 minutes.

To serve 4, you will need:

4 small (10 to 12 oz.) trout
2 to 3 Tbsp. flour
½ tsp. salt
Pinch of pepper

3 to 4 oz. butter
1 tsp. chopped parsley
Juice of 1 lemon
4 oz. blanched almonds, sliced

Clean fish, then wash and dry them. Mix together the flour, salt, and pepper. Dip each fish. Shake to remove surplus. Melt butter in iron skillet. Lay in fish. Sprinkle with chopped parsley and lemon juice. Cook gently until browned, about 5 minutes. Turn and cook other side. Serve with lemon wedge.

DRAWN BUTTER

Gently melt a pound or more of butter till it foams. Let settle. Take off foamy top and then strain into double boiler or pan on back of stovetop. Use on fish, salmon, trout, or vegetables, or on mashed potatoes, etc.

WHITE SAUCE

Melted butter is the foundation for most sauces. For white sauce, melt 2 tablespoons butter; blend in 2 tablespoons flour over low heat. Add salt, then milk gradually, stirring continually until the White Sauce is thickened and smooth.

TARTAR SAUCE

1 c. good mayonnaise (Hellmann's
   or blender homemade)
½ c. finely diced onion
½ c. green pepper relish (put
   through sieve)

Juice of ½ lemon
1 Tbsp. capers or hard-boiled finely
   chopped egg (optional)

Mix all preceding together. Serve with fried fish, fish salads, hard-boiled eggs for salad.

FRENCH DRESSING

1 c. sugar
1 c. vinegar
1 c. salad oil
1 c. catsup

1 tsp. onion salt
1 tsp. celery salt
1 tsp. Worcestershire
1 garlic bud (optional)

Mix together in a quart jar and don't skimp on the sugar. It won't be the same!

BLENDER MAYONNAISE

2 eggs
1¼ c. olive oil
1 tsp. salt
1 tsp. dry mustard

½ tsp. black pepper
2 Tbsp. vinegar (either tarragon or
   wine)

Put eggs in blender. Add enough oil to cover blades. Turn blender on low speed. Add seasoning. Add oil slowly, drop by drop. As mayonnaise becomes thick, turn blender to high. Use all but ¼ cup oil. Add vinegar. (Lemon juice may cause mixture to curdle.) Mayonnaise will now be so thick that you must mix in remaining oil with rubber spatula. This makes about 1¾ cups which must be refrigerated. Use it as a base for adding chives, herbs, etc. Make your own tartar sauce by adding chopped dills, parsley, onion, or for variation, chopped olives and capers.

QUICK BLENDER HOLLANDAISE

Place 3 egg yolks in a blender with 2 teaspoons of lemon juice, ½ teaspoon of salt, and a few grains of cayenne pepper. Turn the blender on and then off once to blend the eggs and seasonings. Quickly melt ¼ pound of sweet butter in a saucepan and heat almost to the boiling point. Turn the blender on high and pour the hot butter steadily into the eggs until the butter is blended and sauce thickened.

BARBECUE SAUCE

1 (14 oz.) bottle catsup
½ c. chili sauce
⅓ c. wine vinegar
¼ c. brown sugar
2 Tbsp. lemon juice
2 Tbsp. Worcestershire sauce

2 Tbsp. prepared mustard
2 Tbsp. cooking oil
2 Tbsp. steak sauce
¼ tsp. salt
¼ tsp. pepper
1 clove garlic, minced

Combine all ingredients in saucepan and simmer for 30 minutes. Great to baste over chicken, pork chops, or leftover pork roast, chopped, and added to sauce for barbeque open sandwich. Makes 2⅔ cups.

WINE SAUCE FOR GAME

You will need half a glass of currant jelly, half a glass of Port wine, half a glass of water, a tablespoon of cold butter, a teaspoonful of salt, the juice of half a lemon, a pinch of cayenne pepper, and 3 cloves. Simmer all together a few minutes, adding the wine after it is strained. A few spoonfuls of the gravy from the game may be added to it. This is excellent with venison or the collops in particular.

COLD BRANDY SAUCE

You will need 2 cupfuls of powdered sugar, half a cupful of butter, 1 wine glass full of brandy, and cinnamon and nutmeg, a teaspoonful of each. Warm the butter slightly and work in the sugar till it comes to a light cream, then add the brandy and spices. Beat it hard and set aside until wanted.

LEMON BRANDY

When you use lemons for punch or lemonade, do not throw away the peels, but cut them in small pieces, the thin yellow outside (not the membrane thick part). Put them in a glass jar or bottle of brandy. You will find this useful for many purposes (For cakes and puddings.)

BROWN SPICE SAUCE
(Steak sauce)

Prep time: 30 minutes. Cooking time: 25 to 30 minutes.

To yield 1 to 1½ pints (U.S. 2½ to 3¾ cups), you will need:

1 lb. shallots, chopped
1 tsp. black pepper
1 Tbsp. black treacle
1 tsp. salt
1 clove garlic, crushed

¼ oz. chillies
1 Tbsp. mushroom ketchup
1 Tbsp. anchovy paste
¼ oz. ground cloves
1 pt. (U.S. 2½ c.) malt vinegar

Put all ingredients into a pan, except vinegar, and just cover with cold water. Boil up and simmer until shallots are reduced to a pulp. Strain through a sieve, pressing well, then return to pan with vinegar. Boil up for 2 to 3 minutes and bottle. If a thicker sauce is liked, add 1 dessert spoon corn flour mixed to a smooth paste with a little vinegar. This is not a long keeping sauce, but will last a few weeks.

BREAD SAUCE

Use 1 cup of stale bread crumbs, 1 onion, 2 ounces of butter, pepper and salt, and a little mace. Cut the onion fine and boil it in milk till quite soft, then strain the milk onto the stale bread crumbs and let it stand an hour. Put it in a saucepan with the boiled onion, pepper and salt, and mace. Give it a boil and serve in a sauce tureen. This sauce can also be used for grouse. Roast partridges are nice served with bread crumbs fried brown in butter with cranberry or currant jelly laid beside them in the platter.

CHILI SAUCE

Boil together 2 dozen ripe tomatoes, 3 green peppers (diced small), a half teaspoon cayenne pepper, 1 large onion (cut fine), and half a cup of sugar. Boil until thick, then add 2 cups of vinegar, then strain the whole. Set back on fire. Add a tablespoonful of salt and a teaspoonful each of ginger, allspice, cloves, and cinnamon. Boil all 5 minutes. Remove and seal in glass jars.

MINT SAUCE NUMBER 1 FOR ROAST LAMB OR CHOPS

Take fresh young spearmint leaves, stripped from stems; wash and drain them or dry on cloth. Chop very fine; put into a gravy boat and to the 3 tablespoons of mint put 2 of white sugar; mix and let it stand a few minutes, then pour over it 6 tablespoons of good cider vinegar or white wine vinegar. This sauce should be made ahead of use. Can stand for ages on the shelf or fridge.

Potatoes and

Vegetables

EQUIVALENT CHART

3 tsp.	1 Tbsp.
2 Tbsp.	⅛ c.
4 Tbsp.	¼ c.
8 Tbsp.	½ c.
16 Tbsp.	1 c.
5 Tbsp. + 1 tsp.	⅓ c.
12 Tbsp.	¾ c.
4 oz.	½ c.
8 oz.	1 c.
16 oz.	1 lb.
1 oz.	2 Tbsp. fat or liquid
2 c.	1 pt.
2 pt.	1 qt.
1 qt.	4 c.
⅝ c.	½ c. + 2 Tbsp.
⅞ c.	¾ c. + 2 Tbsp.
1 jigger	1½ fl. oz. (3 Tbsp.)
8 to 10 egg whites	1 c.
12 to 14 egg yolks	1 c.
1 c. unwhipped cream	2 c. whipped
1 lb. shredded American cheese	4 c.
¼ lb. crumbled Bleu cheese	1 c.
1 lemon	3 Tbsp. juice
1 orange	⅓ c. juice
1 lb. unshelled walnuts	1½ to 1¾ c. shelled
2 c. fat	1 lb.
1 lb. butter	2 c. or 4 sticks
2 c. granulated sugar	1 lb.
3½-4 c. unsifted powdered sugar	1 lb.
2¼ c. packed brown sugar	1 lb.
4 c. sifted flour	1 lb.
4½ c. cake flour	1 lb.
3½ c. unsifted whole wheat flour	1 lb.
4 oz. (1 to 1¼ c.) uncooked macaroni	2¼ c. cooked
7 oz. spaghetti	4 c. cooked
4 oz. (1½ to 2 c.) uncooked noodles	2 c. cooked
28 saltine crackers	1 c. crumbs
4 slices bread	1 c. crumbs
14 square graham crackers	1 c. crumbs
22 vanilla wafers	1 c. crumbs

SUBSTITUTIONS FOR A MISSING INGREDIENT

1 square **chocolate** (1 ounce) = 3 or 4 tablespoons cocoa plus ½ tablespoon fat
1 tablespoon **cornstarch** (for thickening) = 2 tablespoons flour
1 cup sifted **all-purpose flour** = 1 cup plus 2 tablespoons sifted cake flour
1 cup sifted **cake flour** = 1 cup minus 2 tablespoons sifted all-purpose flour
1 teaspoon **baking powder** = ¼ teaspoon baking soda plus ½ teaspoon cream of tartar
1 cup **sour milk** = 1 cup sweet milk into which 1 tablespoon vinegar or lemon juice has been stirred
1 cup **sweet milk** = 1 cup sour milk or buttermilk plus ½ teaspoon baking soda
¾ cup **cracker crumbs** = 1 cup bread crumbs
1 cup **cream, sour, heavy** = ⅓ cup butter and ⅔ cup milk in any sour milk recipe
1 teaspoon **dried herbs** = 1 tablespoon fresh herbs
1 cup **whole milk** = ½ cup evaporated milk and ½ cup water or 1 cup reconstituted nonfat dry milk and 1 tablespoon butter
2 ounces **compressed yeast** = 3 (¼ ounce) packets of dry yeast
1 tablespoon **instant minced onion, rehydrated** = 1 small fresh onion
1 tablespoon **prepared mustard** = 1 teaspoon dry mustard
⅛ teaspoon **garlic powder** = 1 small pressed clove of garlic
1 lb. **whole dates** = 1½ cups, pitted and cut
3 medium **bananas** = 1 cup mashed
3 cups **dry corn flakes** = 1 cup crushed
10 **miniature marshmallows** = 1 large marshmallow

GENERAL OVEN CHART

Very slow oven	250° to 300°F.
Slow oven	300° to 325°F.
Moderate oven	325° to 375°F.
Medium hot oven	375° to 400°F.
Hot oven	400° to 450°F.
Very hot oven	450° to 500°F.

CONTENTS OF CANS

Of the different sizes of cans used by commercial canners, the most common are:

Size:	Average Contents
8 oz.	1 cup
Picnic	1¼ cups
No. 300	1¾ cups
No. 1 tall	2 cups
No. 303	2 cups
No. 2	2½ cups
No. 2½	3½ cups
No. 3	4 cups
No. 10	12 to 13 cups

POTATOES AND VEGETABLES

COMMON POTATO TYPES

Irish potatoes:

New potatoes (spring)　　　　　　**Queens (all-purpose)**
Kerr Pinks (spring)　　　　　　　**Records**
Roosters (boiling)　　　　　　　　**Golden Wonders**

American potatoes:

New potatoes　　　　　　　　　　**Idaho's (baking)**
Red Bliss　　　　　　　　　　　　**Russets**
Maine's (all-purpose)

TO BOIL NEW POTATOES

Do not have the potatoes dug long before they are dressed (impossible in the states because we are all creatures of the supermarket) as they are never as good when they have been out of the ground for some time. Wash them. Rub them and put into boiling, salted water. Let them boil until tender; try them with a fork. When done, pour off the water. Let them stand by the side of the fire with the saucepan lid partially removed, and when they are thoroughly dry, put them into a hot vegetable dish with butter pats on top and serve. If the potatoes are too old to be rubbed, boil them in jackets; drain, peel, and serve as preceding. They will require 20 to 30 minutes to cook.

MASHED POTATOES OR CREAMED POTATOES

Take the quantity needed. Pare and put them into cold water, then put them into a saucepan with a little salt. Cover with water and boil them until done. Drain off the water and mash them fine with a potato masher. Have ready a dollop of butter the size of an egg melted in half a cup of boiling milk and a good pinch of salt; mix it up well, taking care it is not too wet. Put them into a hot vegetable dish. Smooth over the top and dot with butter.

HOME FRIED POTATOES

This recipe literally was made for over 12 years, feeding thousands of hungry Rhode Islanders every week at our 3 restaurants. We boiled up 2 bags potatoes every day. So start with the quantity you need for your recipe. For every 5 or 6 potatoes, use a medium to large onion, peeled and sliced thin.

Put a bit of oil or bacon drippings in frying pan. Add onion, then potato and fry on low heat for a few minutes. Add salt and pepper, ½ usual amount, then Lawry's or other seasoned salt and extra paprika to brown them up. They are wonderful with breakfast, omelettes, or any time of day. We often beat several eggs with a tad of milk in bowl and fold into cooked potatoes in skillet and fold with spatula several times for a wonderful Farmers Omelette.

BROWNED OR DUCHESS POTATOES

Mash them the same as preceding. Put them into an ovenproof dish for serving. Smooth over the top. Brush over with the yolk of an egg, or spread on a bountiful supply of butter and dust with flour. Set the oven to brown. It will take 15 minutes when on quick fire.

OVEN BROWNED POTATOES FOR A ROAST OF BEEF OR LAMB

About ¾ of an hour before ye take your roast out, peel medium size potatoes. Partially boil them, then place them around the roast, basting them with drippings, a generous sprinkle of seasoned salt, and paprika will help them along to brown. Serve them hot around the meat. New potatoes are excellent roasted around the meat.

PEAS AND NEW POTATOES IN CREAM

½ peck peas
2 qt. tiny new potatoes
½ lb. salt pork, diced

1 small onion, minced fine
1 c. thick cream

Shell the peas. Scrub the potatoes well, but do not peel them. Have water boiling in pot large enough to accommodate both peas and potatoes. Drop potatoes into just enough boiling water to cover them. Cook them about 20 minutes while you are trying out the salt pork until it is a delicate color. Skim them out and cook the chopped onion in the fat. The potatoes should now be done. Don't overcook lest they will be mushy. Most of the water should have cooked out. Add the suet and onion to the potatoes. In a separate pan, have a cup of boiling water. Add the peas and cook 3 minutes after the water boils again. Add them with juice to potato casserole. Simmer and add cream.

GAELIC PARSNIP PIE

1 (9 inch) pastry shell
2 lb. fresh parsnips (2 c.), chopped
　　and cooked
1 tsp. salt
2 Tbsp. honey

Pinch of ginger
¼ tsp. cinnamon
1 Tbsp. fresh orange juice
2 tsp. grated rind
2 eggs, slightly beaten

Drain cooked parsnips and cool slightly. Peel and chop finely. Combine in bowl with salt, honey, ginger, cinnamon, orange juice, rind, and eggs. Mix well. Turn into prebaked pastry shell and bake in 375° oven for 30 to 40 minutes. Serve with meat or poultry. Makes 8 servings.

FRESH PARSNIP PATTIES

2 c. mashed, cooked parsnip
1½ tsp. salt
¼ tsp. pepper
1 tsp. sugar
1 tsp. paprika

1 tsp. fresh lemon juice
1 egg
½ c. fine dry bread crumbs
Flour

Combine mashed parsnips, salt, pepper, sugar, paprika, lemon juice, egg, and bread crumbs. Mix well. Shape into 2½ inch patties, ½ inch thick. Dip in flour. Cook in butter or bacon drippings in skillet, turning to brown on both sides. Serve hot with ham, pork, or lamb. Makes 4 to 5 servings.

COLCANNON

6 to 8 spuds	1½ c. milk
2 to 4 oz. butter	Salt and pepper
1 head cabbage (green dark outer leaves)	

Scrub pot and cook in salted water. Quarter head of cabbage core and shred. Put down in very little boiling water. Boil rapidly, turning until cooked. When water is evaporated, peel and mash potatoes with milk. Stir in cabbage and beat well. Taste for seasoning. Serve in warm dish. Hollow center and place in butter.

CHAMP

6 to 8 spuds	1½ c. milk
1 c. chopped spring onions or ½ c. chopped chives	2 to 4 oz. butter
	Salt and pepper

Cook onions in milk. Peel and mash freshly boiled spuds. Mix with milk and onions. Season and serve.

COLCANNON OR BUBBLE AND SQUEAK

Prep time: 15 minutes. Cooking time: 45 minutes.

To serve 4, you will need:

1 lb. mashed potatoes	2 oz. melted butter
1 lb. cooked greens from cabbage, savoy, or kale*	1 medium size onion, chopped, or spring onion

Mix potatoes and chopped greens. Season with salt and pepper if necessary. Heat butter in frying pan; fry onion until transparent, then add potatoes and cabbage. Stir and mix with onions until thoroughly hot. Well grease a casserole and put in the Colcannon. Cover with foil or lid and bake in a hot oven, 400°F. or gas mark 6, for 40 to 45 minutes. Turn out and serve. (Casserole can be well buttered and lined with browned crumbs.) (For variation well packing in Colcannon before baking same method.)

* The darker outer leaves are best. Young spring cabbage before it forms its head is excellent!

BRAISED CELERY

Prep time: 20 minutes. Cooking time: 35 minutes. Serves 4 to 6.

2 large heads celery	4 rashers streaky bacon
Salt and pepper	¼ pt. (U.S. ⅝ c.) thick white sauce
½ pt. (U.S. 1¼ c.) stock	

Trim celery. Cut into quarters and wash well. Put in a well greased shallow ovenproof dish. Sprinkle with salt and pepper. Pour half the stock over celery. Remove rinds from bacon. Fry lightly. Put pieces of bacon on top of celery. Cover closely and bake in hot oven (400°F. or gas mark 6), 30 to 35 minutes or until tender when tested with fork. Take up. Drain well and place on hot dish. Add remaining stock to celery liquor. Boil well to reduce. Make a white sauce with roux and reduced stock. Finish with little milk to whiten. Pour over celery just before serving. Garnish with chopped parsley.

BAKED KIDNEY BEANS

1 lb. dried beans
5 to 6 slices lean rashers
2 large onions, finely chopped
1 green pepper, finely chopped

1 red pepper, finely chopped
2 Tbsp. brown sugar
1 c. catsup
Pinch of salt and pepper

Soak 1 pound kidney beans (red) overnight. Rinse and add fresh water to the bean mixture. Chop or dice rashers and 2 large onions and add pinch of salt and pepper. Cook for 1 to 1½ hours on medium-high heat until almost tender. Pour the mixture into a large baking pan. Add 1 chopped green and 1 chopped red pepper, 1 cup catsup, and 2 tablespoons brown sugar. Bake in preheated oven, 350°F., for 2 hours or until done.

BAKED PARSNIPS

1 lb. parsnips, peeled
½ tsp. salt
2 apples, peeled, cored, and
    chopped

1 c. apple juice
3 Tbsp. brown sugar
⅛ tsp. nutmeg

Trim off tops of the parsnips. Cut in halves lengthwise and remove any woody core. Place in a skillet and cover with water. Add the salt. Bring to a boil and cook until barely tender, about 10 minutes. Drain well and place in a baking dish. Sprinkle with chopped apple and juice with nutmeg and sugar. Bake at 350°F. for 20 minutes or until apples are done. Serves 4 to 6.

GLAZED ONIONS AND CARROTS

1 lb. carrots, peeled and cut into ½
    inch slices
1 (16 oz.) pkg. frozen whole white
    onions or 1 jar boiled onions

¼ c. margarine
2 Tbsp. brown sugar
½ tsp. ground ginger
½ tsp. salt

Place carrots in large saucepan with 1 inch boiling water. Cover and simmer 25 minutes. Add onions. Cover and cook 5 or 10 minutes longer or until vegetables are tender. Drain. Return vegetables to saucepan. Add margarine, brown sugar, ginger and salt, stirring frequently. Cook over medium heat 5 minutes until vegetables are glazed. Makes about 4 cups.

BRAISED RED CABBAGE

1 Tbsp. margarine
1 large onion, chopped (1 c.)
1¼ lb. red cabbage (1 small head),
    cored and thinly sliced
1 Golden Delicious apple, peeled,
    quartered, cored, and thinly
    sliced

½ tsp. salt (if desired)
⅛ tsp. fresh ground black pepper
1 Tbsp. dark brown sugar
1 c. warm water
1 Tbsp. red wine vinegar

1. Melt the margarine in a large skillet, preferably nonstick. Add the onion and saute for 1 minute.

2. Add the cabbage and apple. Continue to cook, stirring. Do not cover or cabbage will turn dark. Add rest of ingredients and continue to simmer until cabbage is cooked. Serve hot or cold.

MARINATED CARROTS

2 lb. carrots, cut in 1 inch long
   diagonal slices
1 large onion, sliced thin rings and
   in halves
1 large green pepper, cut in thin
   strips
1 (10½ oz.) can tomato soup
   (undiluted)

½ c. sugar
½ c. salad oil
1 tsp. salt
1 tsp. pepper
½ c. vinegar

Cook carrots in salted water until just tender. Drain and combine with onions and green pepper. In large bowl, combine soup, oil, vinegar, salt, pepper, and sugar. Bring to boil and stir well to dissolve sugar. Pour hot mixture over vegetables. Cool and serve as a vegetable, salad, or relish. Serves 20 to 30 for side dish.

CORN PUDDING

2 c. fresh corn, scraped off cob
4 eggs, separated
1 c. heavy cream
1 Tbsp. flour

½ Tbsp. sugar
1 tsp. salt
½ tsp. white pepper
¼ tsp. ground mace

Thinly slice off the top of the kernels, then scrape cobs with back of knife or corn scraper. Corn should have a creamy, milky consistency. Beat egg yolks until thick and lemon colored. Stir in cream, flour, sugar, salt, pepper, and mace. Add corn. Beat egg whites until stiff; fold into mixture. Pour into greased 3 quart baking dish. Bake at 350° for 30 minutes or until set. Serves 6.

CABBAGE WITH SOUR CREAM

1 small cabbage
4 Tbsp. butter or margarine
1 egg
1 c. sour cream

2 Tbsp. sugar
1 tsp. prepared horseradish
1 tsp. salt
3 Tbsp. lemon juice

Slice cabbage very thin with sharp knife. Melt butter or margarine in large saucepan or heavy skillet. Add cabbage and cook very slowly until cabbage tastes tender but is still crisp, probably 10 minutes. Better give it an occasional stir. However, beat egg slightly with a fork and stir in sour cream, sugar, horseradish, salt, and pepper. Mix very well, then stir in lemon juice very slowly. When cabbage is cooked, pour sour cream sauce over it and heat very gently. Perfectly delicious with crisp bacon or rasher. Serves 4.

CAULIFLOWER CHEESE

Prep time: 20 minutes. Cooking time: 25 to 30 minutes, including sauce.

To serve 4, you will need 1 medium size cauliflower.

For the sauce:

1 oz. butter	½ level tsp. salt
1 oz. plain flour	Pinch of nutmeg
½ pt. (U.S. 1¼ c.) milk or milk and cauliflower water	3 to 4 oz. Cheddar cheese, grated

Soak cauliflower in cold water for about 15 minutes, then break into flowerets Cook in a little boiling water (salted) in a covered pan until tender and arrange neatl in casserole or a fireproof dish.

For cheese sauce: Melt the butter. Add flour and cook for 1 minute. Remove from heat and add liquid gradually. Bring to the boil, stirring well. Cook for a minute Remove from the heat. Add seasonings and grated cheese and stir until cheese i: melted. Pour over the cauliflower and serve hot.

CREAMED ONIONS

I use jars of store bought baby onions in natural cooking juices. For each jar use a heaping spoonful of margarine, melted, and a spoonful of flour. Cook slowly unti butter is melted and flour added. This should be fairly thick and creamy. Add juice o jarred onions and a bit of milk to whiten the sauce, a dash of salt and pepper, and a taste of nutmeg. Cook until thick and creamy. Add the onions and keep warm unti meal is ready. Can be kept in ovenproof dish in warm oven. Add a crunchy topping o crushed corn flakes and dots of butter and bake on low in oven at 250°F.

MASHED TURNIP

Begin with 1 good size turnip (peeled and diced small). Put into saucepar covered with water. Bring to boil until tender. Drain and put into food processor o mash by hand with potato masher. Add good spoonful of butter or margarine and a pinch of salt and nutmeg and serve in hot dish.

The preceding can be cooked with carrots, peeled and cut up, ½ and ½ or ¾ and ¼ to your taste. Cook and mash and season the same way.

MASHED PARSNIPS

They must be peeled and top and bottom cut off. If very big and woody, par removed. They can be cut up and placed into a saucepan of boiling, salted water anc cooked until tender. Drain and mash as you would turnip or put into food processo for quick spin. Season with a bit of salt, butter, and chopped fresh parsley on top Carrots can be cooked along with parsnip and served mashed also. For this I use ¾ parsnip, ¼ carrot.

BOILED BEETS

Cut green tops off and reserve. Cut off roots and discard. Cover with water ir saucepan and bring to boil, covered, for up to 45 minutes or more depending on size

When knife inserted comes out easy, they are done. Tops can be steamed or sauteed with onions and other greens. They are wonderful served hot with butter or cold with a vinaigrette for salad.

CREAMED CAULIFLOWER

We use a basic cream sauce for this recipe. (Find under Sauces.) However, instead of using all milk, we use half cauliflower water saved from the cooking pot and just enough milk to whiten the sauce and make it creamy. Use fresh chopped parsley for a garnish and pinch of salt and pepper. Also, nutmeg brings out the flavor.

BROCCOLI

This delicate vegetable should be either steamed in a saucepan or wok or boiled in lightly salted water. If steamed when done, we prefer slightly crisp or crunchy. Pour over with lemon juice and extra virgin olive oil and serve right away. This Mediterranean style of serving vegetables is Heart Smart and can be done to any vegetable, cauliflower, broccoli, green onions, spinach, kale, Brussels sprouts, etc.

BRUSSELS SPROUTS

This late summer, early fall veggie is wonderful boiled up in saucepan with pinch of salt. When done strain off water. Add knob of butter and seasoning, either lemon juice or nutmeg and pepper, or olive oil and lemon. Wonderful served with chestnuts roasted and a wonderful pot of beef or pork stew.

SPRING CABBAGE

This wonderful leafy cabbage with its dark green leaves and little or no head is wonderful! Wash and pull apart leaves. Remove all stalks and main hard stems. Tear up leaves and put into pot with little water. Bring to boil. Use ham hocks, salt pork, or drippings for flavor. Cook until tender, 1 or 1½ hours. Serve with bacon and cabbage or ham and cabbage or use for Colcannon.

PICKLED GREEN BEANS

1 large jar with leftover dill pickle
   juice
1 clove garlic
1 tsp. pickling spice

½ c. vinegar
1 lb. whole green beans
1 large onion, sliced

Blanch beans about 3 minutes; mix with onion. Mix remaining ingredients with pickle juice. Add beans and onions. Refrigerate at least 2 to 3 weeks for full flavor.

Notes

Pastry and Sweets

Common Baking Dishes and Pans

Spring Form Pan

Layer Cake or Pie Pan

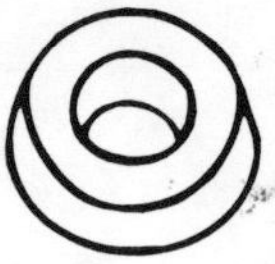

Ring Mold

Baking or Square Pan

Loaf Pan

Brioche Pan

Angel Cake Pan

Bundt Tube

Equivalent Dishes

4-CUP BAKING DISH
= 9" pie plate
= 8" x 1¼" layer cake pan
= 7⅜" x 3⅝" x 2¼" loaf pan

6-CUP BAKING DISH
= 8" or 9" x 1½" layer cake pan
= 10" pie pan
= 8½" x 3⅝" x 2⅝" loaf pan

8-CUP BAKING DISH
= 8" x 8" x 2" square pan
= 11" x 7" x 1½" baking pan
= 9" x 5" x 3" loaf pan

10-CUP BAKING DISH
= 9" x 9" x 2" square pan
= 11¾" x 7½" x 1¾" baking pan
= 15" x 10" x 1" flat jelly roll pan

12-CUP BAKING DISH OR MORE
= 13½" x 8½" x 2" glass baking dish
= 13" x 9" x 2" metal baking pan
= 14" x 10½" x 2½" roasting pan

Total Volume of Pans

TUBE PANS

7½" x 3" Bundt tube	6 cups
9" x 3½" fancy or Bundt tube	9 cups
9" x 3½" angel cake pan	12 cups
10" x 3¾" Bundt tube	12 cups
9" x 3½" fancy tube mold	12 cups
10" x 4" fancy tube mold	16 cups
10" x 4" angel cake pan	18 cups

SPRING FORM PANS

8" x 3" pan	12 cups
9" x 3" pan	16 cups

RING MOLDS

8½" x 2¼" mold	4½ cups
9¼" x 2¾" mold	8 cups

BRIOCHE PAN

9½" x 3¼" pan	8 cups

PASTRY AND SWEETS

BIG JUICY LEMON CAKE FOR CHILDREN TO MAKE

1 box lemon cake mix
4 eggs
1 pkg. lemon instant pudding mix

¾ c. vegetable oil
¾ c. water

Mix all ingredients together for 4 minutes. Bake at 350° in greased 12x15 inch pan for about 30 minutes. When done, top springs back when tapped lightly. While hot, top with icing.

2 c. powdered sugar
⅓ c. orange juice

2 tsp. melted butter

PORTER CAKE

3½ c. flour
1½ c. well packed brown sugar
½ lb. butter
4 eggs
1 tsp. mixed spice
2 c. raisins

2 c. sultanas
1 c. currants
¾ c. chopped peel
⅓ c. Porter
1 tsp. bread soda

Cream butter and sugar. Add sieved flour and beaten eggs. Alternately beat well for 20 minutes. Add rest of ingredients. Dissolve soda in Porter and add it lastly. Bake in slow oven, reg 4, 350°F. for ¾ hour, reg 3 for 2 hours approximately. Finally lower the oven until completely cooked. Keep 1 week before cutting.

ORANGE PAVLOVA

Named in honor of the famed ballerina, Anna Pavlova.

4 egg whites
1 c. sugar
¼ tsp. salt
3 Tbsp. cold water
1 Tbsp. cornstarch
1 tsp. vanilla

1 tsp. grated fresh orange rind
  (peel)
2 tsp. orange juice
2 oranges, peeled and sectioned
¼ c. Triple Sec or Grand Marnier
  (orange flavored liquor)

In large bowl of electric mixer, beat egg whites until soft peaks form. Sprinkle sugar and salt on tops and continue beating until sugar is thoroughly incorporated. Add water and beat well. Add cornstarch and continue beating. Add vanilla, orange peel, and orange juice and beat until whites are glossy and stiff peaks form. Lightly grease a baking sheet and spoon meringue mixture into center, forming an 8 inch free form circle with the spatula.

Smooth sides and top with spatula. If desired, form a raised lip around edges with spatula. Bake at 350°, 15 minutes. Check to see if Pavlova is rising. If so, turn oven off and let Pavlova remain in closed oven for 1 hour. If mixture is not rising after 15 minutes, continue to bake at 350° for another 10 minutes or until it does begin to rise, then turn oven off and let set in oven for 1 hour longer. Place orange sections in small bowl and stir in orange liquor. Let stand while Pavlova bakes.

GREEN APPLE PIE

Peel, core, and slice tart apples enough for a pie; sprinkle over about 3 tablespoonfuls sugar, a teaspoon of cinnamon, a small level tablespoon of sifted flour, 2 tablespoon of water, and a few bits of butter. Stir all together with a spoon. Put into a pie tin lined with pie pastry. Cover with a top crust and bake 40 minutes. The results will be delicious and juicy. Serve with whipped cream, ice cream, or Cheddar cheese.

APPLE BROWN BETTY

2 c. bread crumbs
¼ c. melted butter
6 c. apples, sliced, pared, and cored
½ c. sugar (white or brown), firmly
  packed

½ tsp. nutmeg
¼ tsp. cinnamon
1½ Tbsp. lemon juice or rind
½ c. water

Combine bread crumbs and melted butter and arrange ⅓ mixture in bottom of greased casserole. Cover with half the apples and half the sugar, spice, lemon water mixture. Alternate layers of crumbs, apples, and sugar; top with crumbs. Cover and bake at 375°, ½ hour. Remove cover and bake ½ hour longer or until apples are tender. Serves 6.

Serve warm with cream, whipped cream, or hard sauce.

Hard sauce:

⅓ c. butter or margarine   1 tsp. vanilla
1 c. confectioners sugar   Pinch of salt

Work butter with spoon or beater until creamy. Add sugar gradually. Add vanilla, little at a time. Chill till ready to use.

COLD WATER SPONGE CAKE

6 eggs, separated   2 c. flour
2 c. sugar   ½ c. cold water

Beat yolks and water together. Add sugar and beat till thick and lemon colored. Add flour. In separate bowl, beat egg whites till thick. Fold into preceding batter. Use angel food cake pan. Bake at 350° for about 45 minutes.

SQUASH CAKE

Winter squash or pumpkin.

½ c. shortening   4 tsp. baking powder
1 c. brown sugar   ¼ tsp. baking soda
1 c. white sugar   ½ c. milk
2 beaten eggs   1 c. chopped walnuts
1 c. squash or pumpkin, mashed   1 tsp. maple extract
3 c. flour   Pinch of salt

Cream shortening and slowly add sugar, eggs, and squash. Sift dry ingredients together and add alternately to creamed mixture with milk. Fold in nuts and extract and pour into a greased layer cake pan. Bake at 350° for 30 minutes. Frost with Harvest Moon Frosting or Seven Minute.

HARVEST MOON FROSTING OR SEVEN MINUTE FROSTING

3 egg whites (unbeaten)   ⅜ c. (6 tsp.) water
1½ c. brown sugar   Dash of salt
1 tsp. vanilla

Combine all ingredients, except vanilla, in top of double boiler. Beat well with electric mixer. Place over rapidly boiling water and cook 7 minutes, beating constantly or until frosting will stand in peaks. Remove from boiling water and add vanilla and beat until thick enough to spread. Frost sides then top of cake with frosting for a 3 layer cake.

FRUITED SCRIPTURE CAKE

¾ c. soft butter (Genesis 18:8)
1½ c. sugar (Jeremiah 6:20)
5 eggs, separated (Isaiah 10:14)
3 c. sifted flour (Leviticus 24:5)
¾ tsp. salt (2 Kings 2:20)
3 tsp. baking powder (Amos 4:5)
1 tsp. cinnamon (Exodus 30:23)

¼ tsp. each cloves, allspice, and nutmeg (2 Chronicles 9:9)
¼ c. milk (Judges 4:19)
¾ c. chopped almonds (Genesis 43:11)
¾ c. dried figs, cut (Jeremiah 24:5)
¾ c. raisins (2 Samuel 16:1)

Cream butter with sugar. Beat in egg yolks, 1 at a time. Sift together flour, salt, baking powder, and spices. Blend dry ingredients into creamed mixture alternately with milk. Beat egg whites until stiff and fold in. Fold in chopped almonds, figs, and raisins. Turn into 10 inch tube pan, well greased and dusted with flour. Bake at 325° oven for 1 hour 10 minutes. Cool 10 to 15 minutes and remove from pan. Cool completely and serve with Burnt Sugar Syrup.

BURNT SUGAR SYRUP

1½ c. sugar (Jeremiah 6:20)
½ c. water (Genesis 24:25)

¼ c. butter (Genesis 18:8)

Melt sugar in heavy skillet over low heat. Continue cooking until it is deep amber. Add water and cook until syrup is smooth. Remove from heat. Add butter and stir until melted. Cool and drizzle over top and sides of cake. Decorate with white blanched almonds.

PECAN CRISPS

½ c. butter
1 egg
1 tsp. vanilla

1 c. brown sugar
1 c. flour
1 c. chopped pecans

Mix in order given until smooth. Drop by teaspoon on greased cookie sheet. Bake 6 to 8 minutes at 350°.

OATMEAL SHORTBREAD

1 c. margarine

½ c. brown sugar

Mix until fluffy.

1 tsp. vanilla
1 c. flour

½ tsp. baking soda
2 c. rolled oats

Mix together and add to preceding, then chill. Roll dough ¼ inch thick on floured board. Cut into 1½ inch squares. (May use cookie cutter.) Bake on ungreased cookie sheet for 10 to 12 minutes at 350°. Yield: 3½ to 4 dozen.

Flavor improves if stored in fridge for a few days. Dough will keep up to 2 weeks.

SHORTBREAD

8 c. flour
2 c. butter

1 c. sugar

Place flour and sugar in a bowl. Add butter. Work with hands until it becomes a dough. It should be soft and pliable without being oily or crumbly. Press into 9x13 inch pan and prick with fork. Bake in 375° oven for 35 minutes or until lightly browned. Remove from oven and immediately cut into squares or desired shape. Sprinkle with sugar and let cool.

CHERRY FRUIT SQUARES

½ lb. margarine
1 c. sugar
1 tsp. vanilla
2 eggs
2 c. sifted flour

1 c. nuts, chopped
1 can cherry pie filling (can also use
    fig, date, poppy seed, or any
    other fruit filling)

Cream sugar and margarine; add vanilla. Beat in eggs, 1 at a time. Stir in flour. Add nuts. Spread ¾ of batter in greased 13x9 inch pan. Cover with pie filling. Drop remaining batter by spoonfuls on top. Spread with spatula. Cherries should show through in spots. Bake in 350° oven for 45 minutes. Cool and cut into squares.

CHEESE CAKE

3 well beaten eggs
2 (8 oz.) pkg. cream cheese
1 c. sugar
1 recipe graham nut crust

2 tsp. vanilla
¼ tsp. salt
3 c. sour cream

Combine eggs, cream cheese, sugar, salt, and vanilla. Beat until smooth. Blend in the sour cream and pour into graham shell. Trim with reserved crumbs. Bake at 375° for 35 to 40 minutes or until just set. Cool and chill well 4 to 5 hours. Filling will be soft.

GRAHAM-NUT CRUST

1¾ c. fine graham cracker crumbs
¼ c. finely chopped nuts

¾ tsp. cinnamon
½ c. melted butter

Mix all ingredients together. Reserve 3 tablespoons for topping. Press remainder on bottom and 2½ inches up sides of 9 inch spring pan.

LEMON HEAVEN

Step 1:

2 boxes lemon Jell-O
4 c. boiling water
4 c. diced bananas

1 can crushed pineapple, drained
    and liquid reserved

Dissolve Jell-O in water. Add pineapple and bananas. Let set in refrigerator. Use a 9x13 inch pan.

Step 2:

1 c. pineapple juice	2 Tbsp. cornstarch
2 tsp. butter	¼ c. sugar
1 beaten egg	

Cook over medium heat until thick. Cool and spread over Jell-O.

Step 3: Spread Cool Whip or whipped cream on top. Sprinkle with chopped nuts.

QUICK CHERRY CHEESE CAKE

1 (8 oz.) pkg. cream cheese, softened	2 tsp. sugar
	2 c. Cool Whip
¼ c. softened butter or margarine	1 can cherry pie filling or blueberry

Beat cream cheese with sugar until creamy. Blend in Cool Whip. Pour into graham cracker pie crust. Spread pie filling over top and let chill at least 3 hours.

Graham pie crust: Use 1 cup fine graham cracker crumbs mixed with ¼ cup softened butter.

FESTIVE FRUIT TRIFLE

1 (10½ oz.) loaf angel food cake	½ c. reduced calorie strawberry spread
1½ c. skim milk	
½ c. 1% lowfat cottage cheese	2 Tbsp. Cointreau or orange flavored liquor
¼ c. sugar	
3 Tbsp. cornstarch	5 c. fresh strawberries, hulled and halved
2 Tbsp. instant nonfat dry milk powder	
	5 kiwi fruit, peeled and thinly sliced
1 Tbsp. grated orange rind	4 medium oranges, peeled and sectioned
2 tsp. vanilla extract	

Cut angel food cake into 1 inch cubes. Set aside. Combine milk and next 4 ingredients in container of an electric blender or food processor; top with cover and process until the mixture is smooth. Pour mixture into top of a double boiler. Bring water to boil. Reduce heat to medium-low. Cook, stirring constantly.

DELUXE TRIFLE

1 pkg. vanilla pudding	¾ chilled whipped cream
2 pkg. ladyfingers	3 Tbsp. confectioners sugar
1 pkg. frozen raspberries or strawberries, thawed	⅓ c. sherry
½ c. raspberry jam, strawberry, or red currant jelly	

Cook pudding as directed on package. To assemble, use 9 inch spring pan. Split ladyfingers lengthwise. Spread with jelly and line bottom of pan. Split more ladyfingers and line sides of pan in standing position. Pour ⅓ cup sherry over bottom layer. Pour enough pudding to cover sandwiches. Cover this with layer of fruit, then another layer of pudding and more fruit. Top with whipped cream. If chilled in freezer for 15 minutes before serving, dessert will stand up like pie when cut into servings.

RICE PUDDING

5 Tbsp. raw rice
1 qt. milk
1 Tbsp. butter (heaping)
3 eggs

½ c. sugar
1 tsp. vanilla
1 tsp. salt

Cook rice, milk, and butter in double boiler for 1 hour, stirring occasionally. Beat eggs, sugar, vanilla, and salt together. Combine all ingredients and place in 2 quart greased casserole. Bake in pan of water at 325° for 30 to 50 minutes. Stir every 15 minutes.

ZUCCHINI BREAD PUDDING

2 c. zucchini milk*
¼ c. honey
¼ tsp. salt
2 eggs, slightly beaten
1 tsp. vanilla

1½ c. bread cubes
2 Tbsp. butter
½ tsp. cinnamon
½ c. raisins

Bring zucchini milk to boiling point. Pour over bread cubes. Add butter. Combine honey, salt, and beaten eggs. Add to the bread and milk mixture. Add vanilla, cinnamon, and raisins. Pour into greased casserole and set in a shallow pan of hot water. Bake in 350° oven for about 1 hour (until knife comes out clean).

* Zucchini milk: Peel zucchini, but do not remove seeds or pulp. Cut into chunks about 1 inch in size. Put in blender, filling about ¼ or less full. Switch to liquefy and let run until smooth and zucchini is a liquid. Approximately 2 small zucchini will make 1 cup milk. You may freeze some for later use.

NEVER FAIL PASTRY

5 c. flour
1 Tbsp. salt
2½ c. shortening

1 egg
1 tsp. vinegar
1 c. cold water

Sift flour and salt. Cut in shortening. In a cup, put egg and vinegar. Beat. Add water to make 1 cup. Stir into preceding mixture. Make a ball and chill 1 hour. Makes 2 double and 2 single crusts. Keeps well in refrigerator or freezer.

MAYONNAISE PASTRY

Single crust:

1¼ c. sifted flour
½ tsp. salt
⅓ c. Hellmann's real mayonnaise

¾ tsp. lemon rind (optional)
2 Tbsp. cold water

Mix flour and salt in mixing bowl. Blend in mayonnaise thoroughly with fork. Sprinkle lemon rind and water on top. Mix well. Bake in 475° oven for 8 to 10 minutes.

Double crust:

2 c. sifted flour	1 tsp. lemon rind (optional)
1 tsp. salt	3 Tbsp. cold water
½ c. Hellmann's mayonnaise	

PIE CRUST

Very light and fluffy.

1½ c. flour	½ c. oil
½ tsp. sugar	2 Tbsp. milk
1 tsp. salt	

Combine oil and milk. Whip with whisk. Add flour, sugar, and salt. Continue mixing with fork. Press by hand into 10 inch pie plate. Prick the bottom and sides. Bake at 375° for 15 minutes.

PIE CRUST NUMBER 2
(Regular)

1 c. flour	3 Tbsp. water
⅓ c. Crisco	½ tsp. salt

Cut flour into Crisco until well blended. Add salt and water. Stir until it forms a ball. Roll out on floured board. Bake at 425°F., 20 minutes.

OATMEAL-APPLE CAKE

2 c. flour	5 large apples, peeled and sliced
½ c. rolled oats	1 c. water
¾ c. brown sugar	¾ c. granulated sugar
¾ c. butter or margarine	1 Tbsp. cornstarch
1 tsp. vanilla	

Mix flour, rolled oats, brown sugar, and butter until crumbly. Remove a half cup for topping and line a greased 8 inch pan with remainder. Press sliced apples into dough. Mix water, sugar, cornstarch, and vanilla together and cook until thick. Pour cornstarch mixture over apples and top with remaining half cup of crumbs. Bake in a moderate oven (350°), 20 to 25 minutes. Serve with whipped cream.

APPLE DATE NUT CAKE

1 c. boiling water	1 stick butter or margarine
1 c. chopped dates	1 egg
1 c. chopped apples	1 c. sugar
1 tsp. soda	1½ c. flour
1 tsp. salt	1 c. pecan pieces, broken

Pour water over dates, apples, soda, and salt and let cool. Beat margarine or butter, egg, and sugar until fluffy. Add date-apple mixture to butter mixture. Mix well, then add flour and pecans. Mix well. Bake in 19x13 inch pan (greased) at 350° for 55 minutes.

EASY SPONGE CAKE WITH FRUIT

Sift 1 cup sugar, 1 cup flour, and 2 teaspoonfuls baking powder. Add ½ cup water and 2 egg yolks. Stir well. Beat 2 egg whites and fold in. Pour batter over hot cooked fruit. This can be cherries, blueberries, etc. Cook fruit right in the cake pan, adding a little butter and sugar if necessary. (Don't grease pan.) Bake at 325° about 35 to 40 minutes. Serve with whipped cream.

BLUEBERRY CAKE

1 c. butter
1½ c. sugar
4 eggs
1 c. milk
1 to 2 c. dredged blueberries

3 c. flour, sifted with 2 tsp. baking powder
1 tsp. cinnamon
1 tsp. vanilla

Cream butter and sugar. Add 4 eggs, 1 at a time, beating well. Add flour mixture to egg mixture alternately with milk. Add berries. Butter and flour 2 (9x9 inch) cake pans or 24 muffin tins. Bake square cake 30 to 45 minutes at 350°. Bake muffins at 375° about 20 to 25 minutes.

APPLE COFFEE CAKE

1 c. sugar
1 stick (¼ lb.) margarine
2 eggs
2 c. flour

1 tsp. baking powder
1 tsp. baking soda
½ pt. sour cream
1 tsp. vanilla

Filling:

1 c. chopped walnuts
3 large apples, sliced

¼ c. sugar
1 tsp. cinnamon

Cream sugar, margarine, and eggs until blended. Add dry ingredients, alternating with sour cream. Add vanilla and mix well. In a greased pan, put a layer of dough, then sliced apples. Sprinkle with half the nuts, sugar, and cinnamon. Bake at 350° for 50 to 60 minutes.

OLD-FASHIONED APPLE PUDDING

¼ c. butter or oleo
¾ c. sugar
1 egg
¾ c. milk
3 c. apples, peeled and sliced

2 c. flour
3 tsp. baking powder
1 tsp. salt
1 tsp. vanilla

Cream butter and sugar; sift dry ingredients together. Add dry ingredients alternately with milk. Add vanilla. Stir in apples. Bake at 350° for 40 minutes in a buttered bread pan. Serve warm.

Sauce:

1 Tbsp. butter
¾ c. sugar

2 Tbsp. flour
1 c. boil water (approx.)

Blend together in heavy pan over medium heat. Stir while adding water until thickened.

DEEP DISH APPLE PIE

10 to 12 tart cooking apples (about
    8 c.), cut in small pieces
½ c. sugar
2 Tbsp. lemon juice

1 c. sifted flour
½ c. brown sugar, firmly packed
½ c. (1 stick) butter

Pare apples and cut in small pieces; mix in sugar and lemon juice to coat fruit well; spoon into a 9 inch buttered baking dish. Combine flour and brown sugar in same bowl; cut in butter with pastry blender or 2 knives. Crumble over apples and pat down. Bake in moderate oven, 350°, about 45 minutes or until juice bubbles around edge and crust is golden brown. Serve warm with cream, ice cream, or sharp cheese.

CRAZY FLORENCE
(Apple Pudding with Wine)

1. Peel enough apples to cover the bottom of a baking dish generously. They must be cut into ⅛ pieces and simmered in wine (preferably white) until tender but not soft.
2. Prepare ½ cup bread crumbs and ½ cup finely ground almonds. Add to 3 eggs which have been well beaten with ½ cup sugar.
3. Pour 2 over 1 and on top place slices of buttered bread. Sprinkle liberally with sugar and cinnamon. Bake in a moderate oven until brown.

APPLESAUCE CAKE

Set oven at 350°.

1 c. sugar	½ c. shortening

Cream the sugar and shortening in a bowl.

Sift together and add:

2 c. flour	1 tsp. cinnamon
1 tsp. salt	1 tsp. nutmeg
½ tsp. cloves	

Add:

1 c. chopped dates	1 generous c. unsweetened
½ c. (or more) chopped nuts	applesauce

You can cook up 3 or 4 apples with 1 teaspoon soda dissolved in a little water if no unsweetened sauce is on hand. Bake in a 9x12 inch pan for about 45 minutes or as 2 layers for about 30 minutes.

Plain frosting: With confectioners sugar and with a couple of tablespoons butter, softened, rubbed into it make spreadablelike cream.

CRULLERS

1 c. sugar	3 c. flour
2 Tbsp. melted butter	3 tsp. baking powder
2 eggs	½ tsp. salt
1 c. sweet milk	½ tsp. nutmeg

Mix as soft as can be handled. Roll on a floured board. Cut with a cruller cutter and fry in deep oil.

SPICE CAKE

Combine in order:

2 c. brown sugar	¾ tsp. salt
½ c. melted butter or shortening	1 c. sour milk
1 egg	1 tsp. soda, dissolved in little milk
2 tsp. cinnamon	2 c. flour
1 tsp. cloves	

Butter and flour 2 (8 or 9 inch) square pans. Bake about 25 minutes at 375°.

COOKIES FOR A SÉISŪN

2 c. flour	1½ tsp. baking powder
¼ c. sugar	1 Tbsp. rum
¼ lb. butter	Jam
1 egg	

Cream butter and sugar. Add slightly beaten egg, rum, and flour sifted with baking powder. Mix well. Chill. Roll out and cut into squares. Add jam to each square.

Fold up corners to meet in center. Brush tops with egg white and sprinkle with sugar. Bake on cookie sheet in 350° oven for 15 minutes or golden brown. Serve with pot of hot tea.

PECAN CAKE

This recipe came from a 92 year old lady over a quarter of a century ago. She was Kentucky born and only gave up the recipe when she felt she was too old to make it!

1 lb. sugar
½ lb. butter
6 eggs
1 lb. flour (3¼ c.), sifted
1 tsp. baking powder

2 tsp. nutmeg, sifted with flour and baking powder
1 lb. pecan meats
1½ lb. seeded muscat raisins
1 wine glass good whiskey

Combine ingredients in order. Bake 3 hours at 250° in well greased tube pan with a paper lining on the bottom.

This cake is special and for that special occasion!

MOLASSES-NUT COFFEE CAKE

Mix well:

1 c. brown sugar
1 c. white sugar
1 c. Grandma's molasses
1 c. Crisco and butter (½ and ½)
1 c. strong coffee (the dregs of the pot)
1 c. sour milk
3 tsp. soda, dissolved in milk

1 tsp. cinnamon
1 tsp. nutmeg (scant)
½ tsp. ginger
1 c. raisins
1 c. butternut or walnut meats (salted), dusted in 3 *huge* c. flour

Sift together dry ingredients. Dredge nuts in some of flour. Add dry ingredients alternately with liquid. Stir in raisins and nuts. Grease and flour 2 (8 or 9 inch) square pans. Bake at 365° about 30 to 40 minutes.

SOUR CREAM CAKE

¾ c. sugar
¼ lb. butter
2 eggs
1 c. sour cream

2 c. flour, sifted with baking powder
1½ tsp. baking powder
1 tsp. baking soda
1 tsp. vanilla

Cream butter and sugar. Add eggs, 1 at a time. Add baking soda to sour cream. Alternate flour and sour cream to mixture. Add vanilla.

Sour Cream Cake topping:

½ c. chopped nuts
3 Tbsp. brown sugar

2 tsp. cinnamon
2 Tbsp. melted butter

Pour half of flour mixture into greased 9x9 inch pan. Sprinkle with topping. Add remainder and sprinkle again. Pour melted sweet butter on top. Bake in 375° oven for 45 minutes.

SPONGE CAKE

3 eggs, separated
½ c. boiling water
1 scant c. sugar

1 c. sifted flour
Pinch of salt
1 tsp. vanilla or lemon rind

Beat egg whites until stiff and they stand in soft peaks. Add boiling water to egg yolks and (with same beater), beat until foamy (3 minutes by hand, 1 by electric mixer). Add sugar, then flour and salt. Fold in beaten egg whites and flavoring. Pour into small unbuttered tube pan or a lightly floured 9 inch square pan. Bake at 350° till top springs back when lightly touched with the finger. Invert on wire rack. Let stand till cool. May have to loosen with spatula to ease cake out of pan.

PRUNE AND APRICOT COFFEE CAKE

¾ c. dried prunes
¾ c. dried apricots
⅔ c. light brown sugar, firmly
    packed
1 Tbsp. flour
1 Tbsp. cinnamon
2 c. unsifted flour
2 tsp. baking powder

½ tsp. salt
¾ c. soft shortening
¾ c. granulated sugar
2 eggs
1 tsp. vanilla
¾ c. milk
6 Tbsp. butter, melted
⅓ c. chopped walnuts

1. Let prunes and apricots stand in hot water to cover for 5 minutes. Drain and chop finely. Set aside.
2. Combine brown sugar, 1 tablespoon flour, and cinnamon. Set aside. Sift flour, baking powder, and salt.
3. In large bowl with mixer on high speed, beat shortening, granulated sugar, eggs, and vanilla until light.
4. At low speed, alternately add flour mixture and milk. Beat until just combined.
5. Fold in prunes and apricots.
6. Turn ⅓ batter into greased and floured 9 inch tube pan. Sprinkle with ⅓ brown sugar mixture, then with 2 tablespoons melted butter. Repeat twice. Sprinkle top with walnuts.
7. Bake at 350° for 55 minutes or until cake tester inserted near center comes out clean.

BUTTER CAKE

Bake at 325°F., 60 to 75 minutes.

3 c. flour
1 tsp. salt
1 tsp. baking powder
½ tsp. baking soda
1 c. (2 sticks) oleo or butter
2 c. granulated sugar

4 eggs
1 c. buttermilk
2 tsp. vanilla
¼ c. chopped pecans
Confectioners sugar

For Butter Sauce:

1 c. granulated sugar
¼ c. water

½ c. (1 stick) oleo or butter
2 to 3 tsp. vanilla, orange, or lemon

Cook until butter melts. Grease tube pan. Sprinkle pecans on bottom of pan. Cook sauce. Puncture cake and pour over.

THE GREAT DEPRESSION CAKE

Take away the milk, the eggs, and the butter and what do you have left? A great tasting, moist and spicy cake that became popular after the stock market crash in 1929. Here's a special version.

2 c. sugar	2 tsp. baking powder
2 c. strong coffee	1 tsp. cinnamon
½ c. shortening	1 tsp. allspice
2 c. raisins	1 tsp. cloves
1 apple, peeled and grated	1 tsp. nutmeg
2 c. all-purpose flour	1 c. chopped walnuts
1 tsp. baking soda	

In a large saucepan, simmer the first 5 ingredients for 10 minutes, stirring occasionally. Cool 10 minutes. Blend together the remaining ingredients and stir into mixture. Pour batter into well greased and floured 13x9 inch pan. Bake at 350°F. for 25 to 30 minutes or until toothpick inserted in center comes out clean. Cool and dust with powdered sugar if desired.

Note: Two cups water may be substituted for the coffee. Diced candied fruit and peel may be added for an easy fruit cake.

PEANUT BUTTER COOKIES

½ c. butter flavor Crisco or regular	1 large egg
1 c. creamy peanut butter	1¼ c. flour
¾ c. granulated sugar	¾ tsp. baking soda
½ c. packed light brown sugar	½ tsp. baking powder
1 Tbsp. milk	¼ tsp. salt
1 tsp. vanilla	

Heat oven to 375°F. In large bowl, beat butter flavor Crisco, peanut butter, sugars, milk, and vanilla with electric mixer; add egg and beat well. Stir flour, baking soda, baking powder, and salt together. Add to peanut butter mixture and beat well. Drop rounded tablespoonfuls of dough 2 inches apart onto ungreased baking sheet. Flatten in crisscross pattern with fork dipped in flour. Bake 8 to 10 minutes. Cool 2 minutes on baking sheet. Remove to cooling rack. Makes about 2 dozen cookies.

CHOCOLATE CHIP COOKIES

1¼ c. sifted flour	1 egg
½ tsp. salt	½ tsp. vanilla
½ tsp. soda	1 (6 oz.) pkg. semi-sweet chocolate
½ c. (1 stick) butter or margarine	pieces
½ c. granulated sugar	½ c. chopped pecans (optional)
⅓ c. firmly packed brown sugar	

Heat oven to 375°F. In a small bowl, combine flour, salt, and soda; set aside. Cream butter and sugars. Beat in egg and vanilla. Gradually add flour mixture. Stir in chocolate pieces and pecans. Drop by teaspoonfuls onto lightly greased baking sheets. Bake 10 to 12 minutes. Makes about 2½ dozen cookies.

LUMBER JACK COOKIES

1 c. sugar	1 tsp. soda
1 c. shortening or oil	1 tsp. salt
1 c. dark molasses	2 tsp. cinnamon
2 eggs	1½ tsp. ginger
4 c. sifted flour	1½ tsp. cloves

Cream sugar and shortening. Add molasses and unbeaten eggs. Mix well. Sift together dry ingredients and stir in. Put ¼ cup sugar in a small bowl. Dip fingers into sugar, then pinch off a ball of dough the size of a walnut. Dip into sugar and place balls on a cookie sheet 3 inches apart. Bake at 350°F., 12 to 15 minutes.

LEMON SQUARES

1 c. flour	½ c. margarine
¼ c. confectioners sugar	2 eggs
1 c. granulated sugar	½ tsp. baking powder
¼ tsp. salt	2 Tbsp. lemon juice

Heat oven to 350°. Cream flour, margarine, and confectioners sugar. Press evenly in bottom of 9x9x2 inch square pan. Bake 20 minutes, then beat the remaining ingredients until light and fluffy, about 3 minutes. Pour over hot crust and bake 25 minutes. Cool and cut into 2 inch squares. Makes 16.

OATMEAL CAKE

Combine 1½ cups boiling water and 1 cup oatmeal. Let stand for 20 minutes.

Combine:

1 c. brown sugar	½ c. shortening
1 c. white sugar	2 eggs

Sift together:

1½ c. flour	1 tsp. soda
½ tsp. salt	1 tsp. cinnamon

Add dry ingredients and oatmeal mixture to first mixture. Pour into greased and floured 9 inch square pan. Bake at 350° oven for 35 to 40 minutes. Serve plain or with ice cream or whipped cream.

Or combine:

1 stick margarine	1 c. nuts
1 c. brown sugar	1 c. cocoanut
¼ c. cream or evaporated milk	1 tsp. vanilla

Cook in a saucepan until thick. Pour over cake and put under broiler until brown, approximately 1 minute.

FRUIT SQUARES

2 c. flour   1 tsp. baking powder
1 c. sugar   1 egg
1 stick oleo

Mix well. Spread half the mixture on oblong pan and pat down.

Filling: Cut up 2 cups of figs. Add ½ cup sugar. Cover figs with water. Bring to boil with ½ lemon. Put through food processor. When cooked, cover with remaining mixture, overfilling. Dot with butter. Sprinkle with cinnamon and sugar. Bake at 350°F., ½ hour. Cool before cutting.

SPICE COOKIES

1½ c. soft shortening   ½ tsp. salt
2 c. sugar   2 tsp. cinnamon
2 eggs   1½ tsp. cloves
½ c. molasses (Treakel)   1½ tsp. ginger
4 c. flour   1 to 2 c. raisins
3 tsp. baking soda

Mix together thoroughly shortening, sugar, eggs, and molasses. Sift together and stir in dry ingredients. Add raisins. Drop by teaspoon 2 inches apart onto lightly greased tine. Bake at 350°F. for 10 to 12 minutes.

VINEGAR CAKE

3 c. flour   2 c. water
2 tsp. baking soda   ¾ c. oil
2 c. sugar   2 Tbsp. vinegar
1 tsp. salt   2 tsp. vanilla
6 Tbsp. cocoa

Sift dry ingredients together. Add vinegar, oil, and vanilla. Add water and blend with a fork. Put into a greased 9x13 inch pan. Bake at 350°F. for 30 minutes.

CLOVE CAKE

In a large bowl, cream together 1 cup softened butter and 2¼ cups sugar until the mixture is smooth. In a bowl, beat 5 eggs until they are lemon colored and beat them into the sugar mixture. Into another large bowl, sift together 3 cups sifted flour, 1 tablespoon each of cinnamon and ground cloves, and a pinch of salt. In a small bowl, combine 1 cup buttermilk and 1 tablespoon lemon juice and let mixture stand undisturbed for 5 minutes or until it is thickened.

Add to the sugar mixture ⅓ of the flour mixture and ½ of the milk mixture. Combine the ingredients well. Add another ⅓ of flour mixture and 1 teaspoon baking soda to the remaining milk mixture. Combine the mixture with the sugar mixture and stir in the remaining flour mixture. Pour the batter into a well buttered 10 inch tube pan and bake the cake in a preheated moderate oven at 350°F. for 1 hour or until a cake tester inserted in the center comes out clean. Let the cake cool in the pan on a rack for 10 minutes. Turn the cake out onto the rack and let it cool completely. Sprinkle the cake with sifted confectioners sugar.

CARROT CAKE

Mix 2 cups sugar and 1¼ cups oil. Add 5 grated carrots and 4 eggs (1 at a time). Sift 2 cups flour, 2 teaspoons baking soda, and a dash of salt. Add 1 cup slightly chopped walnuts. Bake in a greased tube pan at 325°F. for 45 to 60 minutes.

Frosting:

1 stick soft butter	1 box confectioners sugar
8 oz. cream cheese	2 tsp. vanilla

WHIPPED CREAM FROSTING

1 c. milk	½ c. shortening
4 Tbsp. flour	1 c. sugar
½ c. butter	2 tsp. vanilla

Cook flour and milk in saucepan until thick. Cool completely. Cream butter and shortening. Add sugar. Add cooked flour mixture to butter mixture. Beat vigorously. Add vanilla.

IRISH POTATO PUDDING

To 2 pounds of potatoes, boiled and mashed, add 1 pound of butter while potatoes are hot. Take 1 pound of white sugar and beat into it 8 eggs. When potatoes cool, add sugar and eggs, then add a half pint of sweet cream. Flavor with half cup of brandy and nutmeg to taste. Bake till golden brown. A good Irish whiskey can be substituted for the brandy.

SUGAR SAVING ICING

1 tsp. gelatin	⅓ c. sugar
¼ c. cold water	½ tsp. vanilla
2 egg whites	

Add gelatin to cold water, then dissolve over hot water. Beat egg whites stiff and gradually add sugar, beating well. Add vanilla and dissolved gelatin, beating constantly.

SUGAR FREE SPANISH CREAM

1 Tbsp. gelatin	3 eggs, separated
¼ c. cold water	1 tsp. Sucaryl
1 c. scalded milk	1 tsp. vanilla

Soften gelatin in cold water for 5 minutes. Add milk. Combine egg yolks and Sucaryl. Add gelatin mixture and cook over hot water 5 minutes, stirring constantly until sugar is dissolved. Cool and chill until slightly thickened. Add vanilla and fold in stiffly beaten egg whites. Turn into mold and chill until firm. Serves 6.

HARD SAUCE

4 oz. butter
2 oz. castor sugar (powdered
   confectioners)

2 Tbsp. brandy or rum

Cream butter and sugar together until quite smooth. Press lumps with spoon. Add brandy or other liquor. Mixture should be thick like paste. Chill before serving. (Ground almonds, 1 ounce, can be added for variation.)

BREAD AND BUTTER PUDDING

Remove crusts from 4 slices of bread, then butter. Cut slices into triangles. Place alternate layers of bread and butter, butter side up, and 1 to 2 tablespoons currants or sultanas to fill a pie dish or ovenware glass dish. Heat ¾ pint (U.S. 1⅞ cups) milk with 1 tablespoon sugar until sugar is melted, then add 2 beaten eggs and ¼ teaspoon vanilla. Pour over bread and fruit. Let it stand 30 to 40 minutes for bread to soak. Grate nutmeg on top. Bake in a moderate oven (350°F. or gas mark 4), for 1 hour until brown and set. Serve with sprinkle of sugar and cream.

EGG CUSTARD

Prep time: 6 to 8 minutes. Cooking time: 8 to 10 minutes. Serves 4.

1 pt. (U.S. 2½ c.) milk
4 tsp. sugar

4 egg yolks
Few drops of vanilla

Warm milk sufficiently to dissolve sugar. Beat the egg yolks and stir into warm milk and sugar. Strain into double boiler. Add flavoring and stir over boiling water in lower part of pan until custard thickens.

JUNKET

Prep time: 5 to 6 minutes. Cooking time: 5 to 6 minutes.

To serve 4, you will need:

1 pt. (U.S. 2½ c.) milk
1 dessert spoon Caster sugar

1½ tsp. rennet
Grated nutmeg

Warm the milk to body heat; test by dipping in the little finger. Temperature is just right if heat cannot be felt. Dissolve sugar in milk, then stir in rennet. Pour into warm dish. Leave junket to set in a warm room. Grate nutmeg on top. For flavoring junkets, add a few drops of vanilla or almond essence after the rennet is added Individual junkets take less time to set.

BRANDIED SPICED PEACHES AND PEARS

Prep time: 15 to 20 minutes. Cooking time: 25 to 30 minutes. Yield: 4 pounds.

Brandy
1 (6 inch) stick cinnamon
¼ oz. ground cloves or whole
¼ oz. whole allspice

1 lb. medium size peaches
1 lb. small size pears
24 oz. sugar
1 pt. (U.S. 2½ c.) water

Do not skin the peaches, but rub the fuzz off them with a cloth dipped in hot water. Cut in halves and remove seeds. Peel the pears, halve, and core as peaches. Boil sugar and water together for 8 minutes. Add spice. Without stirring add the fruit, a few at a time, and cook until tender, about 5 minutes; if the peaches and pears are not covered with syrup, spoon it over them. Remove peaches and pears with a perforated spoon. Can be packed in sterilized jars or kept in cooler in stone crock, covered. Cook the syrup a bit longer to thicken. Measure it and add half amount of brandy, bring to boiling point and pour over fruit. Seal at once or store in covered crock.

CARROT AND APPLE CAKE

2 medium apples, peeled, cored,
   and grated
3 large carrots, peeled and grated
1 Tbsp. lemon juice
4 eggs
1 lb. brown sugar
1½ c. vegetable oil
Grated rind of 1 lemon
1 tsp. baking soda

1 tsp. baking powder
1 Tbsp. vanilla
1 tsp. nutmeg
2 tsp. cinnamon
½ tsp. salt
½ c. milk
3 c. flour, divided
½ c. chopped walnuts or pecans
½ c. golden or regular raisins

Sprinkle apples and carrots with lemon juice. Combine and measure apple and carrot mixture, adding more carrots if necessary to make 2½ cups packed. In large bowl, beat eggs well. Add brown sugar, oil, lemon rind, and apple and carrot mixture. Blend well. Stir in soda, baking powder, vanilla, nutmeg, cinnamon, salt, and milk. Add 1½ cups flour and blend well. Stir in nuts and raisins. Add remaining flour and blend well. Spoon in greased and floured Bundt pan. Bake in preheated oven at 350°F. for 1¼ to 1½ hours. Cool cake in pan 10 minutes, then invert onto serving plate and prepare following frosting.

Cream Cheese Frosting:

6 oz. softened cream cheese
⅓ c. softened butter or margarine
3½ c. powdered sugar

1½ tsp. vanilla
1 tsp. milk (add more milk if needed
   to spread evenly)

RHUBARB CRISP

4 c. rhubarb, washed and diced
1 Tbsp. flour
½ c. sugar
½ tsp. cinnamon

½ top grated orange rind
⅛ tsp. salt
1 Tbsp. water

Mix and put in 8 inch square buttered pan.

Topping:

½ c. brown sugar   ⅓ c. margarine
⅓ c. flour   1½ c. oatmeal (quick cooking)

Mix together and spread on top. Bake at 350°F. for 40 minutes.

RHUBARB COBBLER WITH OATMEAL DUMPLINGS

¾ c. sugar
2 Tbsp. corn starch
1 c. water
½ c. orange juice
1 lb. fresh rhubarb, sliced into 1
    inch pieces (4 c.; frozen may be
    used)
½ c. all-purpose flour

¼ c. whole wheat flour
¼ c. quick cooking oats
1½ tsp. baking powder
½ c. skim milk
2 Tbsp. cooking oil
1 Tbsp. sugar
¼ tsp. cinnamon

In a small saucepan, stir together the ¾ cup sugar and the corn starch. Stir in the water and orange juice. Cook and stir over medium heat until the mixture is bubbly and thickened. Add the rhubarb pieces; cook and stir until the mixture returns to boiling. Remove from heat and cover the mixture to keep warm.

Dumplings: In a medium mixing bowl, stir together flour, whole wheat flour, rolled oats, and baking powder. In a 1 cup glass measuring cup, stir together the skim milk and cooking oil. Add the milk mixture to the flour mixture; stir just until flour mixture is moistened. *Do not* overmix. Transfer rhubarb to 2 quart casserole dish. Spoon dumplings over into 8 mounds on top. Stir remaining cinnamon and sugar together and sprinkle over top. Bake, uncovered, at 425°F. for 20 minutes.

CARRAGEEN MOSS PUDDING

½ c. carrageen or ¼ oz.   2 Tbsp. sugar
3¾ c. milk   Vanilla or lemon peel

Soak moss in tepid water 10 minutes. Wash, drain, and put into a saucepan with milk and lemon peel or vanilla. Bring to a boil and simmer for 20 minutes. Pour through strainer into bowl. Rub all jelly through. Add sugar and chill. Serve with fruit compote or Irish coffee sauce. Serves 6 to 8.

BANANA RHUBARB PIE

¾ c. sugar
2 Tbsp. cornstarch
⅓ c. water
4 c. fresh rhubarb chunks

3 bananas, sliced and gently stirred
    in 2 Tbsp. lemon juice
1 baked 9 inch pie shell

In saucepan, mix sugar and cornstarch. Gradually stir in water till smooth. Add rhubarb. Cook and stir over medium heat until rhubarb is tender, 5 minutes. Layer half the banana slices in pie shell. Add the rhubarb, then top with remaining banana slices. Cool. Serves 6.

RHUBARB PUDDING

5 c. cut up rhubarb
1 c. sugar
1 Tbsp. flour

Cinnamon for flavor
Orange peel for flavor

Mix all together.

Batter over top: Begin with 1 egg, slightly beaten. Add to it 2 tablespoons melted butter or oleo, ½ cup sugar, ½ cup flour, ½ teaspoon baking powder, ¼ teaspoon salt, and ½ cup raisins. Bake at 350° for 35 to 40 minutes.

Aunt Florence Wilburn-Dudley

RHUBARB CUSTARD PIE

2 c. diced rhubarb
1 c. sugar
2 eggs, separated
1 c. milk
2 Tbsp. flour

¼ tsp. salt
1 tsp. lemon juice
¼ c. sugar
1 (9 inch) unbaked pie shell

Stew the rhubarb with ¾ cup sugar and a splash of water until soft. Cool. Add the milk and the yolks of the eggs, beaten with ¼ cup sugar, flour, and salt. Add the lemon juice. Pour into the unbaked pie shell. Flute rim to stand above pie plate. Bake in a 450°F. oven for 10 minutes, then 325°F. for 25 minutes. Beat the egg whites until stiff, adding the remaining ¼ cup sugar gradually. Beat until glossy. Spread the meringue on the pie and return to a 300°F. oven for 10 minutes or until lightly browned.

FLOATING ISLANDS

2 eggs, separated
2 c. scalded milk
A pinch of salt

1 Tbsp. Sucaryl
1 tsp. vanilla
4 Tbsp. powdered sugar

Beat egg yolks well. Add a little hot milk to them and stir, then pour yolks into 2 cups of hot milk and mix well. Pour into top part of double boiler and cook only until liquid coats spoon, no longer. Cool quickly and add salt, Sucaryl, and vanilla. Beat egg whites until stiff. Add 4 tablespoons powdered sugar to egg whites, 1 tablespoon at a time, beating after each addition. Pour custard into dessert dishes and put egg whites on top of each. Garnish with favorite jam, jelly, or fruit.

Notes

Jams, Jellies, Chutneys, Curds, and Liquors

APPLE VARIETIES

NAME	SEASON	COLOR	FLAVOR/TEXTURE	EATING	PIE
Astrachan	July-Aug	Yellow/ Greenish Red	Sweet	Good	Good
Baldwin	Oct-Jan	Red/ Yellowish	Mellow	Fair	Fair
Cortland	Oct-Jan	Green/Purple	Mild, tender	Excel.	Excel.
Delicious, Red	Sept-June	Scarlet	Sweet, crunchy	Excel.	Good
Delicious, Golden	Sept-May	Yellow	Sweet, semifirm	Excel.	Excel.
Empire	Sept-Nov	Red	Sweet, crisp	Excel.	Good
Fameuse	Sept-Nov	Red	Mild, crisp	Excel.	Fair
Granny Smith	Apr-Jul	Green	Tart, crisp	V. Good	V. Good
Gravenstein	July-Sept	Green w/red stripes	Tart, crisp	Good	Good
Ida Red	Oct	Red	Rich	Good	Good
Jonathan	Sept-Jan	Brilliant red	Tart, tender, crisp	V. Good	V. Good
Macoun	Oct-Nov	Dark red	Tart, juicy, crisp	Excel.	Good
McIntosh	Sept-June	Green to red	Slightly tart, tender, juicy	Excel.	Excel.
Newtown Pippin	Sept-June	Green to red	Slightly tart, firm	V. Good	Excel.
Northern Spy	Oct	Red	Crisp, tart	V. Good	V. Good
Rhode Island Greening	Sept-Nov	Green	Very tart, firm	Poor	Excel.
Rome Beauty	Oct-June	Red	Tart, firm, slightly dry	Good	V. Good
Stayman-Winesap	Oct-Mar	Red	Semifirm, sweet, spicy	V. Good	Good
Winesap	Oct-June	Red	Slightly tart, firm, spicy	Excel.	Good
Yellow Transparent	July-Aug	Yellow	Tart, soft	Poor	Excel.

JAMS, JELLIES, CHUTNEYS, CURDS, AND LIQUORS

LEMON CURD NUMBER 1

Prep time: 20 minutes. Cooking time: 15 minutes.

To yield 1 pound, you will need:

4 oz. butter
8 oz. granulated sugar

3 eggs
Grated rind and juice of 2 lemons

Melt butter in top of double boiler saucepan placed over low heat. Add sugar slowly and stir until well blended. Beat eggs and pour them gradually into the butter and sugar. Stir until mixture is light and creamy; do not allow it to get very hot. Grate the peel from the lemons. Add to mixture. Squeeze the juice from the lemons and add it slowly, stirring all the time. Place the pan over boiling water in bottom of double boiler over low heat and stir until curd forms a film on back of spoon. Pour into a screw-top jar. Yields 1 pound.

LEMON CURD NUMBER 2

Can be used for small tarts or a filling, or a filling for a layer cake, or on toast!

1 c. butter
1½ c. sugar
Grated rind of 2 lemons

½ c. fresh lemon juice
5 eggs, beaten

Put all the ingredients in the top of a double boiler over hot water. Cook, stirring constantly, until nearly thick. Cover and continue cooking for 10 minutes. Cool and store in refrigerator in a covered jar. Makes 3 cups.

Did you know? Traditional coarse cut bitter marmalade which is part of every Irish breakfast table is made from Seville oranges which are at their best during January and February, but marmalade can be made from any citrus fruits, sweet oranges, grapefruit, and lemons. One of my favorites is 3 fruit marmalade made from lemon, orange, and grapefruit. However, some of the sweeter varieties are best served at tea time.

COARSE CUT MARMALADE

Prep time: 1 to 1½ hours, plus overnight soaking. Cooking time: 2½ to 2¾ hours.

To yield 9 to 10 pounds, you will need:

3 lb. Seville oranges
1 sweet orange
2 lemons

6 pt. (U.S. 15 c.) water
Pinch of bicarbonate of soda
6 lb. Demerara sugar

Wash fruit. Cut into quarters. Remove loose pith. Cut up fruit coarsely or put through mincer, catching all the juice and removing pips; put pips in separate basin. Cover them with ½ pint (U.S. 1¼ cups) water. Cover chopped fruit with remaining water and soda; leave overnight. Transfer all to preserving pan; add water from pips. Put pips in muslin bag and suspend from handle of pan so bag tests in the water.

Simmer 2 to 2½ hours or until fruit is soft enough to disintegrate when pressed between finger and thumb. Remove bag of pips, pressing out all liquid dissolved, then bring quickly to the boil. Keep at a steady rolling boil for 10 minutes, then test for a set by putting a spoonful on a cold plate. It should form a soft jelly that wrinkles when pushed with the forefinger. Boil longer if necessary, but 20 minutes should be sufficient. Put into hot jars. Cover with paraffin wax when cold.

RHUBARB GINGER JAM

Prep time: 20 minutes. Cooking time: 50 minutes.

To yield 5 to 6 pounds, you will need:

4 lb. red rhubarb	**4 large lemons**
4 lb. sugar	**8 oz. crystallized ginger**

Wash rhubarb and cut into 1 inch pieces. Place it in a casserole with a quarter of the sugar. Cover it and cook in a cool oven (310°F. or gas mark 2) until soft but not broken, 15 to 20 minutes, then put rhubarb in preserving pan with rest of sugar and lemon juice and cut up ginger. Boil steadily until jam sets, about 30 minutes, and just before jam is finished add the grated rind of lemon. Put into hot jars and cover at once.

BLACK CURRANT JELLY

Prep time: 15 to 20 minutes. Cooking time: 30 minutes plus overnight straining.

To yield 2 pints (U.S. 5 cups), you will need:

3 lb. black currants	**Sugar**
1½ to 2 pt. (U.S. 3¾ to 5 c.) water	

Wash currants; there is no need to remove stalks. Just cover with water and simmer until tender, mashing well. Strain and allow 1 pound sugar to 1 pint (U.S. 2½ cups) juice. Stir over low heat until sugar dissolves; boil quickly until a good set is reached. Pour into heated jars. Tie down when cold.

SPICED APPLE JELLY

Prep time: 1 hour. Cooking time: 1 hour 20 minutes, plus overnight straining.

To yield 1¾ to 2 pints (U.S. 4⅜ to 5 cups), you will need:

4 lb. cooking apples	**1 (3 inch) stick cinnamon**
1 to 1½ pints (U.S. 2½ to 3¾ c.)	**6 whole cloves**
water	**Sugar**

Wash and weigh apples after removing bruised parts. Cut them up roughly. Just cover with water. Add spices. Simmer 1 hour, stirring often. Strain through jelly bag or flannel overnight. Measure juice. Allow 1 pound sugar to each pint (U.S. 2½ cups). Stir over low heat until sugar dissolves; boil quickly until a good set is reached. See preceding for testing, about 15 minutes. Pour into heated jars; tie down when cold.

MINT SAUCE

Prep time: 20 to 25 minutes. Cooking time: 5 to 10 minutes.

To yield 1½ pints (U.S. 3¾ cups), you will need:

8 oz. mint leaves · 12 oz. sugar
1 pt. (U.S. 2½ c.) vinegar Pinch of powdered Borax

Wash, dry, and chop finely the freshly gathered mint. Boil the vinegar with the sugar and Borax until sugar dissolves. Half fill bottles with mint. Fill up with cooled vinegar. The bottles should have screw tops or very tight fitting corks. Dip the necks of the bottles in melted paraffin wax to be sure they are airtight.

RHUBARB STRAWBERRY CONSERVE

2 c. pink rhubarb, cut in ½ inch 4 c. sugar
pieces ¼ tsp. ginger
3 c. small whole strawberries 1 c. golden seedless raisins
1 c. diced pineapple (no juice)
Thin peel, cut fine, and juice 2
oranges

If you cannot get golden seedless raisins, use extra strawberries or pineapple. Ordinary raisins darken the finished product too much. Mix fruit, orange juice, sugar, and ginger in a large shallow enamel pan and let them stand several hours. Set the pan into the oven at 375° and cook for 1 hour. Now, cook the conserve on top of the stove till the juice thickens on a cold saucer. This amount fills 6 (6 ounce) glasses, plus what was lifted during the finished stage to put on your favorite whatever, with a cuppa.

YELLOW TOMATO JAM

4 lb. yellow tomatoes 5 lb. sugar
5 oranges

Grind tomatoes and oranges; mix with sugar and boil until thick and clear. Fill jelly jars. When cool cover with paraffin.

STRAWBERRY JAM
(Cooked)

1 qt. strawberries 1 lemon, peeled and quartered
3½ c. sugar 1 tsp. butter

Clean and wash berries. Add sugar, lemon, and butter. Bring to a rolling boil and boil for 9 minutes, stirring constantly. Remove from heat and stir for 3 more minutes. Place into sterilized jars and seal. No paraffin necessary.

STRAWBERRY JAM
(Freezer)

8 c. berries, cleaned and mashed 5 c. sugar

Mix and let stand 20 minutes. Boil 1 cup water and add 1 package Sure-Jell and boil for 2 minutes. Add to berries and stir in containers and let stand 24 hours (no longer). Put in freezer. Keeps for 2 years.

OVERNIGHT STRAWBERRY JAM

2 qt. strawberries, washed and
   hulled

6 c. sugar
2 Tbsp. lemon juice

Cover berries with boiling water and let stand 2 minutes. Drain. Add lemon juice and 4 cups of sugar. Place over heat and bring to boil and boil for 2 minutes. Remove. Add remaining 2 cups sugar. Continue to boil for 5 minutes. Skim off foam. Pour mixture into platters to a depth of ¼ inch and let stand overnight. Next morning, scrape into jars and seal.

PLUM CONSERVE

2 qt. plums
4½ c. sugar
1½ lemons

1½ oranges
3 c. raisins
1½ c. chopped walnuts

Wash plums; cover with water and cook until tender. Remove seeds and chop; measure 6 cups of pulp. Add sugar, juice, and grated rind of lemons and oranges. Add raisins and cook until thick and clear. Add nuts and pour into sterilized jelly glasses. Pour paraffin over top to seal.

DILL PICKLES

Wash small cucumbers and pack in quart jars, either whole or sliced lengthwise.

For each quart:

2 cloves garlic
Several sprigs dill
2 Tbsp. salt

2 c. water
1 c. vinegar

Bring to boil and pour over pickles. Seal and cold pack for 5 minutes. Allow 2 months before using.

CORN RELISH

12 large ears corn
1 qt. ripe tomatoes, peeled
1 qt. onions
2 green peppers, chopped
2 red peppers, chopped

4 c. sugar
3 c. vinegar
2 tsp. turmeric
2 Tbsp. salt

Boil 1 hour in large, heavy kettle, stirring frequently. Add a paste made of 2 tablespoons flour mixed with vinegar. Boil until thick. Put in pint jars and seal.

APPLE CHUTNEY

10 tart apples (3½ lb.), sliced
2 to 3 c. cider vinegar
3½ c. brown sugar
1 c. chopped onion
¼ lb. garlic, minced
1 sweet red pepper, chopped
1 hot pepper, minced, or 1 to 2 tsp.
   dried

½ c. white raisins
½ c. seedless raisins
½ c. dried currants
¼ lb. candied ginger, sliced
1 tsp. ground ginger
4 Tbsp. Worcestershire sauce

All measurements are "about." It is a matter of taste, but don't skimp on garlic or ginger. Combine ingredients and bring to slow boil. Simmer slowly, stirring often, until a good consistency. It will take a while, but the apples should keep their shape. Seal in jars. However, it keeps well refrigerated unsealed.

RASPBERRY SAUCE

12 oz. frozen unsweetened
   raspberries or fresh
¼ c. apple juice

2 tsp. cornstarch
1 Tbsp. fructose

Combine all ingredients, except fructose, and cook over medium heat until sauce thickens, about 10 minutes. Remove from heat and stir in fructose. Serve warm. Yield 1 cup.

IRISH COFFEE SAUCE

1 c. sugar
⅓ c. water

1 c. coffee
1 Tbsp. Irish whiskey

Make caramel by dissolving ⅓ cup water and 1 cup sugar over heat and cook until caramel. Remove; pour in 1 cup coffee. Continue to cook. Add whiskey last and cool.

Note: Can be kept in covered jar in fridge for weeks.

SPANISH POINT CHOCOLATE SAUCE

We serve this over ice cream or with pound cake and cream.

1 c. fresh, cold water
2 sq. bitter chocolate, cut up
1 c. raw sugar

Pinch of salt
1 Tbsp. butter
1 tsp. vanilla extract

Put water and chocolate into heavy saucepan directly over heat. *Low!* Stir constantly until thickened. Add remaining ingredients.

IRISH WHISKEY SAUCE

½ c. Irish whiskey
½ c. soft butter or margarine
4 c. light brown sugar, firmly packed

2 eggs
2 c. light cream
Dash of nutmeg

With electric mixer at medium speed, beat butter with sugar until creamy in top of double boiler. Beat in eggs, cream, and nutmeg; beat until mixture is fluffy. Cook, stirring occasionally, over hot, hot boiling, water until mixture is thickened. Remove from heat. Gradually stir in whiskey. Serve warm or cold. Excellent over plum pudding, open apple tart, or suet pudding. Makes 5 cups. Serves 6 to 8.

KITCHEN PRAYER

Lord of pots and pans and things. Since I've not time to be a saint by doing lovely things or watching late with thee or dreaming in the dawn light or storming Heaven's gates, make me a saint by getting meals and washing up the plates. Although I must have Martha's hands, I have a Mary mind and when I black the boots and shoes, thy sandals, Lord, I find. I think of how they trod the earth. What time I scrub the floor. Accept this meditation, Lord. I haven't time for more.

Klara Munkres

KAHLUA

Boil 4 cups sugar and 4 cups water for 10 minutes. Add ¾ cup instant coffee, 1 vanilla bean (cut up), and 1 fifth of vodka. Shake daily for 3 weeks in a gallon jug. Strain and bottle. Keeps without refrigeration.

HOMEMADE COINTREAU

1 bottle poteen   **½ lb. brown sugar**
4 whole oranges, washed and stuck   **½ jar honey**
**   with cloves (5 or 6 each)**

Seal in jar for 3 weeks. Strain and bottle.

DANDELION WINE

1 gal. dandelion blossoms   **3 lb. sugar**
1 gal. water (boiling)   **1 oz. yeast**
3 oranges and 3 lemons, cut in
**   small pieces**

Pick dandelion flowers early in the morning, taking care not to get a particle of the bitter stem attached. Pour boiling water over the flowers. Let stand 3 days. Strain. Add the rest of the ingredients. Let stand to ferment 3 weeks. Strain and bottle.

RHUBARB RASPBERRY WINE

8 lb. pink to red rhubarb	1 Tbsp. gelatin
2 pkg. frozen raspberries	1 c. lukewarm water
8 qt. boiling water	8 lb. sugar
1 yeast cake	

Wash rhubarb. Slice in ¼ inch pieces. Add the raspberries. Put the fruit in a large enamelware kettle. Pour boiling water over the fruit. Cover. Let stand 3 days, then dissolve yeast and gelatin in lukewarm water. Strain liquid off the fruit into a stoneware crock. Add yeast, gelatin, and sugar. Stir until sugar is dissolved. Cover crock and let mixture stand 3 days longer. Pour into sterilized jugs. Put into a cool place, the cellar has an even temperature, and leave it for 3 months, then strain through sterilized cheesecloth. Put into clean soda bottles. Press sterilized caps down firmly. Label and date.

DOG BISCUITS

For your furry friend.

Sift together:

3½ c. all-purpose flour	2 c. bulgur
2 c. whole wheat flour	1 c. corn meal
1 c. rye flour	½ c. instant nonfat dry milk
4 tsp. salt	

Sprinkle 1 envelope dry yeast over ¼ cup very warm water. Add 2 or 3 cups beef broth to flour mixture. Mix everything together with hands. Mixture will be stiff. Add more broth if necessary. Roll out onto floured surface to ¼ inch thick. Put on ungreased baking sheet. Brush with mixture of 1 egg and 1 tablespoon milk. Cut into shapes. Bake at 300° for 45 minutes. Turn oven off and let it remain in oven overnight. Makes 1½ dozen.

EUROPEAN MEASURE		AMERICAN CUPS
5 oz.	Sliced Apple	1 cup
4½ oz.	Icing Sugar	1 cup (sifted)
4 oz.	Cheddar Cheese	1 cup (grated)
3½ oz.	Cocoa	1 cup
2½ oz.	Desiccated Coconut	1 cup
2 oz.	Fresh Breadcrumbs	1 cup
1 oz.	Plain Dessert Chocolate	1 square
¼ oz.	Dried Yeast	1 packet
¼ oz.	Gelatine	1 tablespoon
¾ tablespoon	Gelatine	1 envelope
½ oz.	Flour	1 level tablespoon*
1 oz.	Flour	2 level tablespoons
1 oz.	Sugar	1 level tablespoon
½ oz.	Butter	1 level tablespoon smoothed off
1 oz.	Golden Syrup or Treacle	1 level tablespoon
1 oz.	Jam or Jelly	1 level tablespoon

* must be standard U.S. measuring tablespoon

METRIC EQUIVALENTS

It is difficult to convert to French measures with absolute accuracy, but 1 oz. is equal to approximately 30 grammes, 2 lb. 3 oz. to 1 kilogramme. For liquid measure, approximately 1¾ English pints may be regarded as equal to 1 litre, ½ pint to 3 decilitres (scant); 3½ fluid oz to 1 decilitre.

OVEN TEMPERATURES

DESCRIPTION OF OVEN	APPROXIMATE TEMPERATURE CENTRE OF OVEN °F	THERMOSTAT SETTING
Very Slow or Very Cool	200–250	¼ = 240 ½ = 265 1 = 290
Slow or Cool	250–300	2 = 310
Very Moderate	300–350	3 = 335
Moderate	350–375	4 = 350
Moderately Hot		5 = 375
to Hot	375–400	6 = 400
Hot to Very Hot	425–450	7 = 425
Very Hot	450–500	8 = 450 9 = 470

Note: This table is an approximate guide only. Different makes of cooker vary and if you are in doubt about the setting it is as well to refer to the manufacturer' temperature chart.

HANDY CONVERSION TABLE

EUROPEAN MEASURE	(Approximate conversion table)	AMERICAN CUPS
1 lb.	Butter or other fat	2 cups
1 lb.	Flour (sifted)	4 cups
1 lb.	Granulated or Castor Sugar	2¼ cups
1 lb.	Icing or Confectioners' Sugar	3½ cups
1 lb.	Brown (moist) Sugar	2¼ cups
1 lb.	Golden Syrup or Treacle	1⅓ cup
1 lb.	Rice	2¼–2½ cups
1 lb.	Dried Fruit (chopped)	2–2½ cups
1 lb.	Raw Chopped Meat (finely packed)	2 cups
1 lb.	Lentils or Split Peas	2 cups
1 lb.	Coffee (unground)	2½ cups
1 lb.	Dry Breadcrumbs	4 cups
8 oz.	Butter or Margarine	1 cup
8 oz.	Lard	1 cup
7 oz.	Castor Sugar	1 cup
7 oz.	Soft Brown Sugar	1 cup (packed)
7 oz.	Candied Fruit	1 cup
6⅓ oz.	Chopped Dates	1 cup
6 oz.	Chocolate Pieces	1 cup
5 oz.	Currants	1 cup
5½ oz.	Cooked Rice	1 cup
5¾ oz.	Seedless Raisins	1 cup
5 oz.	Candied Peel	1 cup
5 oz.	Chopped Mixed Nuts	1 cup

Notes

Notes

Notes

INDEX OF RECIPES

JAMS, JELLIES, CHUTNEYS, CURDS, AND LIQUORS

KITCHEN HINTS

If you've over-salted soup or vegetables, add cut raw potatoes and discard once they have cooked and absorbed the salt.

A teaspoon each of cider vinegar and sugar added to salty soup or vegetables will also remedy the situation.

If you've over-sweetened a dish, add salt.

A teaspoon of cider vinegar will take care of too-sweet vegetable or main dishes.

Pale gravy may be browned by adding a bit of instant coffee straight from the jar . . . no bitter taste, either.

If you will brown the flour well before adding to the liquid when making gravy, you will avoid pale or lumpy gravy.

A different way of browning flour is to put it in a custard cup placed beside meat in the oven. Once the meat is done, the flour will be nice and brown.

Thin gravy can be thickened by adding a mixture of flour or cornstarch and water, which has been mixed to a smooth paste, added gradually, stirring constantly, while bringing to a boil.

Lumpless gravy can be your triumph if you add a pinch of salt to the flour before mixing it with water.

A small amount of baking soda added to gravy will eliminate excess grease.

Drop a lettuce leaf into a pot of homemade soup to absorb excess grease from the top.

If time allows, the best method of removing fat is refrigeration until the fat hardens. If you put a piece of waxed paper over the top of the soup, etc. it can be peeled right off, along with the hardened fat.

Ice cubes will also eliminate the fat from soup and stew. Just drop a few into the pot and stir; the fat will cling to the cubes; discard the cubes before they melt. Or, wrap ice cubes in paper towel or cheesecloth and skim over the top.

If fresh vegetables are wilted or blemished, pick off the brown edges, sprinkle with cool water, wrap in paper towel and refrigerate for an hour or so.

Perk up soggy lettuce by adding lemon juice to a bowl of cold water and soak for an hour in the refrigerator.

Lettuce and celery keep longer if you store them in paper bags instead of cellophane.

To remove the core from a head of lettuce, hit the core end once against the counter sharply. The core will loosen and pull out easily.

Cream will whip faster and better if you'll first chill the cream, bowl, and beaters well.

Soupy whipped cream can be saved by adding an egg white, then chilling thoroughly. Rebeat for a fluffy surprise!

A few drops of lemon juice added to whipping cream helps it whip faster and better.

Cream whipped ahead of time will not separate if you add ¼ teaspoon unflavored gelatin per cup of cream.

A dampened and folded dish towel placed under the bowl in which you are whipping cream will keep the bowl from dancing all over the counter top.

Brown sugar won't harden if an apple slice is placed in the container.

But if your brown sugar is already brick-hard, put your cheese-grater to work and grate the amount you need.

KITCHEN HINTS

A slice of soft bread placed in the package of hardened brown sugar will soften it again in a couple of hours.

Potatoes will bake in a hurry if they are boiled in salted water for 10 minutes before popping into a very hot oven.

A leftover baked potato can be rebaked if you dip it in water and bake in a 350° oven for about 20 minutes.

A thin slice cut from each end of the potato will speed up baking time as well.

You'll shed less tears if you'll cut the root end off of the onion last.

No more tears when peeling onions if you place them in the deep freeze for four or five minutes first.

Scalding tomatoes, peaches, or pears in boiling water before peeling makes it easier on you and the fruit — skins slip right off.

Ripen green fruits by placing in a perforated plastic bag. The holes allow air movement, yet retain the odorless gas which fruits produce to promote ripening.

To hasten the ripening of garden tomatoes or avocados, put them in a brown paper bag, close the bag and leave at room temperature for a few days.

When pan frying always heat the pan before adding the butter or oil.

A little salt sprinkled into the frying pan will prevent spattering.

Meat loaf will not stick if you place a slice of bacon on the bottom of the pan.

Vinegar brought to a boil in a new frying pan will prevent foods from sticking.

Muffins will slide right out of tin pans if the hot pan is first placed on a wet towel.

No sticking to the pan when you're scalding milk if you'll first rinse the pan in cold water.

Add a cup of water to the bottom portion of the broiling pan before sliding into the oven, to absorb smoke and grease.

A few teaspoons of sugar and cinnamon slowly burned on top of the stove will hide unpleasant cooking odors and make your family think you've been baking all day!

A lump of butter or a few teaspoons of cooking oil added to water when boiling rice, noodles, or spaghetti will prevent boiling over.

Rubbing the inside of the cooking vessel with vegetable oil will also prevent noodles, spaghetti, and similar starches from boiling over.

A few drops of lemon juice added to simmering rice will keep the grains separate.

Grating a stick of butter softens it quickly.

Soften butter for spreading by inverting a small heated pan over the butter dish for a while.

A dip of the spoon or cup into hot water before measuring shortening or butter will cause the fat to slip out easily without sticking to the spoon.

Before measuring honey or other syrup, oil the cup with cooking oil and rinse in hot water.

Catsup will flow out of the bottle evenly if you will first insert a drinking straw, push it to the bottom of the bottle, and remove.

If you wet the dish on which the gelatin is to be unmolded, it can be moved around until centered.

KITCHEN HINTS

A dampened paper towel or terry cloth brushed downward on a cob of corn will remove every strand of corn silk.

An easy way to remove the kernels of sweet corn from the cob is to use a shoe horn. It's built just right for shearing off those kernels in a jiffy.

To determine whether an egg is fresh, immerse it in a pan of cool, salted water. If it sinks, it is fresh; if it rises to the surface, throw it away.

Fresh eggs' shells are rough and chalky; old eggs are smooth and shiny.

To determine whether an egg is hard-boiled, spin it. If it spins, it is hard-boiled; if it wobbles and will not spin it is raw.

Egg whites won't run while boiling or poaching if you'll add a little vinegar to the water.

Eggs will beat up fluffier if they are allowed to come to cool room temperature before beating.

For baking, it's best to use medium to large eggs; extra large eggs may cause cakes to fall when cooled.

Egg shells can be easily removed from hard-boiled eggs if they are quickly rinsed in cold water first.

For fluffier omelets, add a pinch of cornstarch before beating.

For a never fail, never weep meringue, add a teaspoon of cornstarch to the sugar before beating it into the egg whites.

Once your meringue is baked, cut it cleanly, using a knife coated with butter.

A meringue pie may be covered with waxed paper or plastic wrap with no fear of sticking, if you'll first grease the paper with oleo.

No "curly" bacon for breakfast when you dip it into cold water before frying.

Keep bacon slices from sticking together; roll the package into a tube shape and secure with rubber bands.

A quick way to separate frozen bacon: heat a spatula over a burner, slide it under each slice to separate it from the others.

Cheese won't harden if you'll butter the exposed edges before storing.

A cloth dampened with vinegar and wrapped around cheese will also prevent drying out.

Thaw fish in milk. The milk draws out the frozen taste and provides a fresh-caught flavor.

When browning any piece of meat, the job will be done more quickly and effectively if the meat is very dry and the fat is very hot.

You'll get more juice from a lemon if you'll first warm it slightly in the oven.

Popcorn will stay fresh and you will eliminate "old maids" if you store it in the freezer.

Running ice cold water over the kernels before popping will also eliminate "old maids".

After flouring chicken, chill for one hour. The coating adheres better during frying.

Empty salt cartons with spouts make dandy containers for bread crumbs. A funnel is used for getting the crumbs into the carton.

A sack of lumpy sugar won't be if you place it in the refrigerator for 24 hours.

CLEANUPS

Fill blender part way with hot water; add a drop of detergent; cover and turn it on for a few seconds. Rinse and drain dry.

Loosen grime from can openers by brushing with an old toothbrush. To clean blades, run a paper towel through the cutting process.

Don't panic if you accidentally scorch the inside of your favorite saucepan. Just fill the pan halfway with water and add ¼ cup baking soda. Boil awhile until the burned portions loosen and float to the top.

A jar lid or a couple of marbles in the bottom half of a double-boiler will rattle when the water gets low and warn you to add more before the pan scorches or burns.

To remove lime deposits from teakettles, fill with equal parts vinegar and water. Bring to a boil and allow to stand overnight.

Before washing fine china and crystal, place a towel in the bottom of the sink to act as a cushion.

To remove coffee or tea stains and cigarette burns from fine china, rub with a damp cloth dipped in baking soda.

To quickly remove food that is stuck to a casserole dish, fill with boiling water and 2 tablespoons of baking soda or salt.

To clear a sink or basin drain, pour ½ cup of baking soda followed by a cup of vinegar down the drain . . .let the mixture foam, then run hot water.

When a drain is clogged with grease, pour a cup of salt and a cup of baking soda followed by a kettle of boiling water.

Silver will gleam after a rubbing with damp baking soda on a soft cloth.

For a fast and simple clean-up of your hand grater, rub salad oil on the grater before using.

A toothbrush works great to clean lemon rind, cheese, onion, etc. out of the grater before washing it.

While baking fruit pies, does the juice runneth over? Shake salt into the spills. They'll burn to a crisp and can be easily scraped up with a spatula.

Grease splatters or other foods that have dried on the stove, burner rings, counter appliances, etc., may be removed by applying dry baking soda to the spots, then rubbing with a damp cloth. Rinse with clear water, dry and enjoy the like-new look.

CALORIE COUNTER

Almonds:
roasted in oil, salted, 9-10 nuts 62
Apple butter, 1 tbsp. 33
Apple juice, canned or bottled, 1 cup 117
Apples:
fresh, with skin, 1 average (2½" diameter) 61
dried, cooked, sweetened, ½ cup 157
dried, cooked, unsweetened, ½ cup 100
applesauce, canned, sweetened, ½ cup 116
applesauce, canned, unsweetened, ½ cup 50
apricot nectar, canned or bottled, 1 cup 143
apricots:
fresh, 3 average (12 per lb.) 55
canned, 4 halves with 2 tbsp. heavy syrup 105
canned, water pack, ½ cup with liquid 38
asparagus:
canned, drained, cut spears, ½ cup 25
frozen, 6 spears 23
avocados, 3⅛" diameter 185

bacon, fried, drained, 2 medium slices 86
bacon, Canadian, fried, drained, 1 slice 58
bagel, egg or water, 1 medium (3" diameter) 165
bamboo shoots, raw, cuts, ½ cup 21
bananas, 1 average 118
bean sprouts, soy, raw, ½ cup 24
beans, baked, canned:
with pork and tomato sauce, ½ cup 156
beans, green or snap:
fresh, boiled, drained, cuts or French style, ½ cup . . 16
canned, with liquid, ½ cup 22
beans, lima, immature seeds:
boiled, drained, ½ cup 95
canned, with liquid, ½ cup 88
beans, pea, navy, or white, dry, cooked, ½ cup 112
beans, red kidney, canned, with liquid, ½ cup 115
beef, choice grade cuts (without bone):
brisket, lean only, braised, 4 oz. 253
chuck, arm, lean only, pot-roasted, 4 oz. 219
club steak, lean only, broiled, 4 oz. 277
flank steak, lean only, pot-roasted, 4 oz. 222
ground, lean (10% fat), broiled, 4 oz. 248
porterhouse steak, lean only, broiled, 4 oz. 254
rib, lean only, roasted, 4 oz. 273
round steak, lean only, broiled, 4 oz. 214
rump, lean only, roasted, 4 oz. 236
short plate, lean only, simmered, 4 oz. 253
sirloin steak, double-bone, lean only, broiled, 4 oz. . 245
sirloin steak, round-bone, lean only, broiled, 4 oz. . 235
T-bone steak, lean only, broiled, 4 oz. 253
beef, corned:
boiled, medium-fat, 4 oz. 422
canned, lean, 4 oz. 211
beef and vegetable stew, canned, 4 oz. 90
beets:
boiled, drained, sliced, ½ cup 33
blackberries:
fresh, ½ cup 42
canned, juice pack, ½ cup with liquid 68
blueberries:
fresh, ½ cup 45
canned, water pack, ½ cup with liquid 47
bologna, all meat, 4 oz. 315
boysenberries:
canned, water pack, ½ cup with liquid 45
frozen, unsweetened, ½ cup 30
braunschweiger (smoked liverwurst), 4 oz. 362
brazil nuts (3 large nuts) 90
bread, commercial:
Boston brown, 1 slice 101
cracked wheat, 1 slice, 20 per loaf 60
French, 1 slice 44
Italian, 1 slice 28

pumpernickel, 1 slice 79
raisin, 1 slice, 20 per loaf 60
rye, light, 1 slice, 20 per loaf 56
white, firm-crumb type, 1 slice, 20 per loaf 63
whole wheat, firm-crumb type, 1 slice, 20 per loaf . . 56
Bread stuffing, mix, mixed with butter, water, ½ cup . 250
Broccoli:
raw, 1 large spear 32
boiled, drained, cut spears, ½ cup 20
Brussels sprouts boiled, drained ½ cup 28
Butter, 1 Tbsp. 100
Butter, whipped, 1 tbsp. 67

Cabbage:
red, raw, chopped or shredded, ½ cup 14
white, raw, chopped or shredded, ½ cup 11
Cake, mix, prepared as directed on package:
angelfood, without icing, 3½-oz. serving 269
coffee cake, 3½-oz. serving 322
devil's food, with chocolate icing, 3½-oz. serving . . 369
white, with chocolate icing, 3½-oz. serving 351
yellow, with chocolate icing, 3½-oz. serving 365
Candies, 1-oz. serving:
almonds, chocolate-covered 161
butter mints, after dinner (Kraft) 106
butterscotch 112
cherries, dark chocolate-covered (Welch's) 115
chocolate, milk 147
chocolate, semi-sweet 144
coconut, chocolate-covered 124
fudge, chocolate, with nuts 121
gum drops 98
jelly beans 104
licorice (Switzer) 101
Life Savers, all flavors except mint 111
Life Savers, mint 108
mints, chocolate-covered 116
marshmallows (Campfire) 100
peanut brittle 119
peanut cluster, chocolate-covered (Kraft) 151
raisins, chocolate-covered 120
toffee, chocolate (Kraft) 111
Cantaloupe, fresh, ½ melon, 5" diameter 58
Carrots:
raw, 1 average 21
boiled, drained, diced, ½ cup 23
Catsup, tomato, bottled, 1 tbsp. 16
Cauliflower:
raw, flowerbuds, sliced, ½ cup 12
boiled, drained, flowerbuds, ½ cup 14
Celery, raw, 1 outer stalk (8" long) 7
Cereals:
All-bran, 1 cup 192
bran, 100% (Nabisco), 1 cup 150
bran flakes, 40%, 1 cup 106
bran flakes with raisins, 1 cup 144
corn flakes, 1 cup 97
corn flakes, sugar coated, 1 cup 154
Cream of Wheat, cooked, 1 cup 133
farina, quick-cooking, cooked, 1 cup 105
oat flakes (Post), 1 cup 165
oatmeal or rolled oats, cooked, 1 cup 132
rice, puffed, 1 cup 60
wheat flakes, 1 cup 106
wheat, puffed, 1 cup 54
wheat, puffed, presweetened, 1 cup 132
wheat, shredded, 1 biscuit (2½" x 2" x 1¼") 89
Cheese:
American, processed, 1 oz. 105
blue or Roquefort type, 1 oz. 104
brick, 1 oz. 105
cheddar, domestic, 1 oz. 113
cottage, creamed, small curd, ½ cup 112

CALORIE COUNTER

cream, 1 tbsp. ... 52
cream, whipped, 1 tbsp. ... 37
Gouda, 1 oz. ... 108
Monterey Jack, 1 oz. ... 103
Mozzarella, part-skim, 1 oz. ... 85
Muenster, 1 oz. ... 100
Neufchatel (Borden's), 1 oz. ... 73
Old English, processed, 1 oz. ... 105
Parmesan, grated, 1 Tbsp. ... 23
pimiento, American, processed, 1 oz. ... 105
Provolone, 1 oz. ... 99
ricotta, moist, 1 oz. ... 45
Romano, 1 oz. ... 110
Roquefort, 1 oz. ... 105
Swiss, domestic, 1 oz. ... 104
Cheese food, American, processed, 1 oz. ... 92
Cherries:
  sweet, fresh, whole, ½ cup ... 41
Cherries, maraschino, bottled, 1 oz. with liquid ... 33
Chestnuts, fresh, 10 average ... 141
Chicken:
  broiled, meat only, 4 oz. ... 154
  roasted, dark meat, 4 oz., no skin ... 204
  roasted, light meat, 4 oz., no skin ... 207
Chili, with beans, canned ½ cup ... 170
Chili, without beans, canned, ½ cup ... 255
Coconut:
  dried, sweetened, shredded, ½ cup ... 258
Cod (meat only):
  broiled, with butter, fillets, 4 oz. ... 192
  frozen, fish sticks, breaded, 5 sticks, 4 oz. ... 276
Coffee, prepared, plain, 1 cup ... 2
Coleslaw, commercial, with mayonnaise, ½ cup ... 87
Cookies, commercial:
  brownies, from mix, with nuts and water, 1 oz. ... 114
  butter thins, 1 piece (2" diameter) ... 23
  chocolate chip, 1 piece (2¼" diameter) ... 50
  coconut bar, 1 oz. ... 140
  fig bar, 1 average piece ... 50
  gingersnaps, 1 piece (2" diameter) ... 29
  graham cracker, plain, 1 piece (5" x 2½") ... 55
  ladyfinger, 1 piece ... 40
  macaroon, 1 piece (2¾" diameter) ... 91
  oatmeal with raisins, 1 piece (2⅝" diameter) ... 59
  peanut sandwich, 1 piece (1¾" diameter) ... 58
  shortbread, 1 average piece ... 37
  vanilla wafer, 1 piece (1¾" diameter) ... 19
Corn:
  boiled, drained on cob, 1 ear (5" x 1¾") ... 70
  boiled, drained, kernels, ½ cup ... 69
  canned, cream style, ½ cup ... 105
Corn chips (Fritos), 1 oz. ... 166
Crackers:
  bacon-flavor, 1 oz. ... 127
  butter, round, 1 piece (1⅞" diameter) ... 15
  cheese, round, 1 piece (1⅝" diameter) ... 17
  Melba toast, white, regular, 1 piece ... 15
  Rye-Krisp, 1 piece (1⅞" x 3½") ... 21
  saltines, 1 piece ... 12
  whole wheat, 1 oz. ... 114
Cranberry juice cocktail, canned or bottled, 1 cup ... 164
Cranberry sauce, canned, strained, ½ cup ... 202
Cream:
  half and half, ½ cup ... 162
  sour, 1 tbsp. ... 26
  whipping, light, ½ cup unwhipped ... 358
  whipping, heavy, ½ cup, unwhipped ... 419
Cream substitute, non-dairy, dry, 1 tbsp. ... 33
Cucumber, with skin, 1 large (8¼" long) ... 45

Dates, domestic, 10 average ... 219
Duck, domestic, roasted, meat only, 4 oz. ... 352

Eclair, custard filled, with chocolate icing, 1 average . 239
Eggnog, 8% fat (Borden's), ½ cup ... 171
Eggplant, boiled, drained, diced, ½ cup ... 19
Eggs, chicken:
  boiled or poached, 1 large egg ... 82
  fried, with 1 tsp. butter, 1 large egg ... 99
  scrambled, with 1 tsp. butter, 1 large egg ... 111
Endive, raw, 10 small leaves ...
Escarole, raw, 1 large leaf ...

Fat, vegetable shortening, 1 tbsp. ... 11
Figs:
  dried, 1 large fig (2" x 1") ... 5
Fish cakes, fried, frozen, reheated, 4 oz. ... 30
Flour:
  all-purpose, sifted, 1 cup ... 41
  buckwheat, dark, sifted, 1 cup ... 32
  cake or pastry, sifted, 1 cup ... 34
  rye, dark, unsifted, 1 cup ... 41
  wheat, self-rising, sifted, 1 cup ... 40
Frankfurters, all-meat, 1 average (10 per lb.) ... 13
Fruit cocktail, canned, water pack, ½ cup with liquid . . 4
Fruit, mixed, frozen, sweetened, 4 oz. ... 12

Gelatin dessert, flavored, prepared with water, ½ cup . 7
Gooseberries, fresh, ½ cup ... 3
Grape drink, canned, 1 cup ... 13
Grape juice, canned or bottled, 1 cup ... 16
Grapes:
  fresh (Concord, Delaware, etc.), 10 ... 1
  fresh (Thompson seedless, etc.), 10 ... 3
Grapefruit juice:
  canned, sweetened, 1 cup ... 13
  canned, unsweetened, 1 cup ... 16

Haddock, fried, breaded fillets, 4 oz. ... 18
Halibut, fillets, broiled with butter, 4 oz. ... 19
Halibut, frozen, steak, 4 oz. ... 25
Halibut, smoked, 4 oz. ... 25
Ham:
  boiled, packaged, 4 oz. (about 4 slices) ... 26
  fresh, medium-fat, roasted, 4 oz. ... 42
  picnic, cured, medium-fat, roasted, 4 oz. ... 36
  canned, cured, lean only, roasted, 4 oz. ... 2
  canned, deviled, 4 oz. ... 3
Herring:
  canned, plain, 4 oz. with liquid ... 2
  pickled, Bismark-type, 4 oz. ... 2
  smoked, hard, 4 oz. ... 3
Hickory nuts, shelled, 4 oz. ... 7
Honey, strained or extracted, 1 tbsp. ...
Honeydew melon:
  fresh, 1 wedge (2" x 7") ...

Ice cream:
  hardened, rich, 16% fat, ½ cup ... 1
  soft-serve (frozen custard), ½ cup ... 1
Ice cream bar, chocolate coated, 3-oz. bar ... 1
Ice cream cone, sugar 1 cone ...
Ice cream cone, waffle, 1 cone ...
Ice milk, hardened, 5.1% fat, ½ cup ... 1
Ice milk, soft-serve, 5.1% fat, ½ cup ... 1
Ice milk bar, chocolate coated, 3-oz. bar ... 1

Jams and preserves, all flavors, 1 tbsp. ...
Jellies, all flavors, 1 tbsp. ...

Kale:
  fresh, leaves only, 4 oz. ...
  fresh, with stems, boiled, drained, ½ cup ...
Knockwurst, 1 link (4" x 1⅛" diameter) ...
Kumquats, fresh, 1 average ...

CALORIE COUNTER

amb, retail cuts:
  chop, loin, lean only, broiled, 2.3 oz. with bone 122
  leg, lean and fat, roasted, boneless, 4 oz. 317
  shoulder, lean only, roasted, boneless, 4 oz. 233
eeks, raw, 3 average 52
emon juice:
  fresh, 1 tbsp. 4
emonade, frozen, diluted, 1 cup 107
emons, fresh, 1 average (2⅛" diameter) 20
entils, whole, cooked, 1 cup 212
ettuce:
  iceberg, 1 leaf (5" x 4½") 3
  romaine, 3 leaves (8" long) 5
mes, fresh, 1 average (2" diameter) 19
verwurst, fresh, 4 oz. 348
bster, cooked in shell, whole, 1 lb. 112
bster, cooked or canned, meat only, cubed, ½ cup . 69

acadamia nuts, 6 average nuts 104
acaroni, boiled, drained, ½ cup 96
acaroni and cheese, canned, ½ cup 114
ackerel, fresh or frozen, broiled with butter, 4 oz. . . 268
angos, whole, 1 average (1½ per lb.) 152
argarine, salted or unsalted, 1 tbsp. 102
armalade, citrus flavors, 1 tbsp. 51
lk, chocolate, canned, with skim milk, 1 cup 190
lk, chocolate, canned, with whole milk, 1 cup 213
lk, cow's:
  whole, 3.5% fat, 1 cup 159
  buttermilk, cultured, 1 cup 88
  skim, 1 cup 88
  skim, partially, 1 cup 145
  canned, condensed, sweetened, 1 cup 982
  canned, evaporated, unsweetened, 1 cup 345
  dry, whole, 1 tbsp. dry form 35
  dry, nonfat, instant, 1 envelope (3.2 oz.) 327
lk, malted, beverage, 1 cup 244
ffin, corn, mix, made with egg, milk, 1.4 oz. muffin 130
shrooms, raw, sliced, chopped or diced, ½ cup . . . 10
shrooms, canned, with liquid, ½ cup 21
stard greens, boiled, drained, ½ cup 16

ctarines, fresh, 1 average (2½" diameter) 88
odles, chow-mein, canned, ½ cup 110
odles, egg, cooked, ½ cup 100

, cooking or salad:
  orn, safflower, sesame or soy, 1 tbsp. 120
  live or peanut, 1 tbsp. 119
ves, pickled, canned or bottled:
  reen, 10 large (¾" diameter) 45
  ipe, salt-cured, Greek style, 10 extra large 89
ons, mature:
  aw, 1 average (2½" diameter) 40
  aw, chopped, 1 tbsp. 4
nge juice:
  esh, California, Valencia, 1 cup 117
  esh, Florida, Valencia, 1 cup 112
  anned, sweetened, 1 cup 130
  anned, unsweetened, 1 cup 120
  ozen, concentrate, unsweetened, diluted, 1 cup . 112
nges, fresh, 1 average 71

cakes, prepared from mix as directed on package:
  ain and buttermilk, 4" diameter cake 61
  uckwheat and other flours, 4" diameter cake 54
  aya juice, canned, 1 cup 120
  ayas, fresh, whole, 1 papaya (3½" x 5⅛") 119
  ch nectar, canned, 1 cup 120
  esh, 1 average 38
  anned, in juice, 2 peach halves with 2 tbsp. juice . . 45
  ied, ½ cup 210

Peanut butter, commercial, 1 tbsp. 94
Peanuts:
  roasted, in shell, 10 nuts 105
  roasted, chopped, 1 tbsp. 52
Pear nectar, canned, 1 cup 130
Pears:
  fresh, Bartlett, 1 pear (2½" diameter) 100
  canned, in heavy syrup, 1 pear half and 2 tbsp. syrup 71
  dried, ½ cup 241
Peas, green:
  boiled, drained, ½ cup 57
Peas, split, cooked, ½ cup 115
Pecans:
  shelled, 10 large nuts 62
  chopped, 1 tbsp. 52
Peppers, hot, chili:
  green, raw, seeded, 4 oz. 42
  green, chili sauce, canned, ½ cup 25
  red, chili sauce, canned, ½ cup 26
Peppers, sweet, green:
  raw, fancy grade, 1 pepper (3" diameter) 36
Peppers, sweet, red:
  raw, fancy grade, 1 pepper (3" diameter) 51
Perch, ocean, Atlantic, frozen, breaded, 4 oz. 382
Perch, white, raw, meat only, 4 oz. 134
Pickle relish:
  hamburger (Heinz), 1 tbsp. 17
  sweet, 1 tbsp. 21
Pickles, cucumber:
  dill, 1 large (4" long) 15
  sweet gherkins, 1 small (2½" long) 22
Pies, frozen:
  apple, baked, 3⅛" arc (⅛ of 8" pie) 173
  cherry, baked, 3⅛" arc (⅛ of 8" pie) 211
  coconut custard, baked, 3⅛" arc (⅛ of 8" pie) 187
Pimientos, canned, drained, 1 average 10
Pineapple:
  fresh, sliced, 1 slice (3½" diameter x ¾") 44
  canned, heavy syrup, chunks or crushed, ½ cup . . . 95
  canned, water pack, tidbits, ½ cup with liquid 48
Pineapple juice, canned, unsweetened, 1 cup 138
Pistachio nuts, chopped, 1 tbsp. 53
Plums:
  damson, fresh, whole, 10 plums (1" diameter) 66
  canned, purple, 3 plums and 2¾ tbsp. liquid 110
Popcorn:
  popped, plain, 1 cup 23
  popped, with oil and salt added, 1 cup 41
Pork:
  Boston butt, lean only, roasted, 4 oz. 279
  chop, lean only, broiled, 4 oz. with bone 308
  loin, lean only, roasted, 4 oz. 288
Potato chips, 10 chips (2" diameter) 114
Potato sticks, ½ cup 95
Potatoes, white:
  baked, in skin, 1 long 145
  boiled, in skin, 1 round 104
  fried, ½ cup 228
  frozen, hash brown, cooked, ½ cup 174
  mashed, with milk and butter, ½ cup 99
Potatoes, sweet:
  baked in skin, 1 average 161
  boiled, in skin, 1 average 172
  boiled, in skin, mashed, ½ cup 146
  candied, 1 piece (2½" long x 2") 176
Pretzels, commercial varieties:
  rods, 1 pretzel (7½" long) 55
  twisted, 3-ring, 10 pretzels 117
Prune juice, canned or bottled, 1 cup 197
Prunes, dried, medium-size, 1 average 16
Pumpkin, canned, ½ cup 41
Radishes, raw, whole, 10 medium 8
Raisins, seedless (½ cup) 210

CALORIE COUNTER

Raspberries:
black, fresh, ½ cup 49
red, fresh, ½ cup 35
canned, black, water pack, 4 oz. with liquid 58
canned, red, water pack, ½ cup with liquid 43
frozen, red, sweetened, ½ cup 123
Rhubarb, cooked, sweetened, ½ cup 191
Rice, cooked (hot):
brown, long grain, ½ cup 116
white, long grain, ½ cup 112
white, parboiled, long grain, ½ cup 93
Rolls and buns, commercial (ready to serve):
frankfurther or hamburger, 1.4 oz. roll 119
hard, rectangular, ⅞-oz. roll 78
raisin, 1-oz. roll 78
sweet, 1-oz. roll 89
whole wheat, 1-oz. roll 73

Salad dressings, commercial:
blue cheese, 1 tbsp. 76
French, 1 tbsp. 66
Italian, 1 tbsp. 83
mayonnaise, 1 tbsp. 101
Roquefort cheese, 1 tbsp. 76
Russian, 1 tbsp. 74
Thousand Island, 1 tbsp. 80
Salami:
cooked, 1 slice (4" diameter) 68
dry, 1 slice (3⅛" diameter) 45
Salmon, smoked, 4 oz. 200
Sauces:
barbecue, 1 tbsp. 17
soy, 1 tbsp. 12
tartar, 1 tbsp. 74
tomato, canned (Hunt's), ½ cup 35
Sauerkraut, canned, ½ cup with liquid 21
Sausages:
polish, 2.7 oz. sausage (5⅜" long x 1" diameter) .. 231
pork, cooked, 1 link (4" long x ⅞" diameter) 62
pork, cooked, 1 patty (3⅞" diameter x ¼") 129
pork and beef, chopped, 4 oz. 383
Vienna, canned, 1 sausage (2" long) 38
Sherbet, orange, ½ cup 130
Shrimp:
fresh, breaded, fried, 4 oz. 255
canned, drained, 10 medium shrimp 37
Soft drinks:
cola, 1 cup 96
cream soda, 1 cup 105
fruit flavored (citrus, cherry, grape, etc.), 1 cup 113
root beer, 1 cup 100
Seven-Up, 1 cup 97
Soup, canned, condensed, diluted with equal part water:
asparagus, cream of, 1 cup 65
beans with pork, 1 cup 168
beef broth, bouillon or consomme, 1 cup 31
beef noodle, 1 cup 67
celery, cream of, 1 cup 86
chicken consomme, 1 cup 22
chicken, cream of, 1 cup 94
chicken gumbo, 1 cup 55
chicken noodle, 1 cup 62
chicken vegetable, 1 cup 76
chicken with rice, 1 cup 48
clam chowder, Manhattan type, 1 cup 81
minestrone, 1 cup 105
mushroom, cream of, 1 cup 134
onion, 1 cup 65
pea, split, 1 cup 145
tomato, 1 cup 88
vegetable beef, 1 cup 78
vegetarian vegetable, 1 cup 78

Spaghetti:
plain, boiled 8-10 minutes, drained, ½ cup 9
canned, in tomato sauce with cheese, ½ cup 9
canned, with meatballs in tomato sauce, ½ cup ... 12
Spinach:
boiled, drained, leaves, ½ cup 2
Squash, summer:
scallop variety, boiled, drained, sliced, ½ cup 1
yellow, boiled, drained, sliced, ½ cup 1
zucchini, boiled, drained, sliced, ½ 1
Squash, winter:
acorn, baked, ½ squash (4" diameter) 8
acorn, boiled, mashed, ½ cup 4
butternut, baked, mashed, ½ cup 7
butternut, boiled, mashed, ½ cup 5
Strawberries:
fresh, whole, ½ cup 2
canned, water pack, ½ cup with liquid 2
Sugar, beet or cane:
brown, ½ cup firm packed 41
brown, 1 tbsp. firm packed 5
granulated, ½ cup 38
granulated, 1 tsp. 1
powdered, unsifted, ½ cup 23
powdered, stirred, 1 tbsp. 3
Sunflower seed kernels, in hull, ½ cup 12
Sunflower seed kernels, hulled, ½ cup 40
Syrups:
chocolate, thin-type, 1 tbsp. ....
corn, light or dark, 1 tbsp. ....
maple, 1 tbsp. ....
molasses, blackstrap, 1 tbsp. ....
molasses, light, 1 tbsp. ....
molasses, medium, 1 tbsp. ....
sorghum, 1 tbsp. ....

Tangerines, fresh, 1 average (2⅜" diameter) ....
Tomato juice, canned or bottle, 1 cup ....
Tomato juice cocktail, canned or bottled, 1 cup .....
Tomato paste, canned, ½ cup 1
Tomato puree, canned ½ cup ....
Tomatoes, ripe:
raw, whole, 1 average (about 2⅖" diameter) ....
canned, ½ cup with liquid ....
Toppings: dessert:
butterscotch, 1 tbsp. ....
caramel, 1 tbsp. ....
chocolate fudge, 1 tbsp. ....
pineapple, 1 tbsp. ....
Tuna, canned:
in oil, solid pack or chunk style, drained, ½ cup ... 1
in water, all styles, with liquid, 4 oz. ....
Turkey:
dark meat, roasted, 4 oz. 2
light meat, roasted, 4 oz. 2
canned, boned, ½ cup 2
Turnip greens:
fresh, boiled in small amount water, drained, ½ cup .
Turnips, boiled, drained, cubed, ½ cup ....

Vegetable juice cocktail, canned, 1 cup ....
Vegetables, mixed, frozen, boiled, drained, ½ cup ...

Waffles, baked from mix:
made with egg and milk, 1 round (7" diameter) 2
Walnuts, 10 large nuts ....
Watermelon, with rind, 1 wedge (4" x 8") ....
Wheat bran, commercially milled, 4 oz. ....
Wheat germ, toasted, 1 tbsp. ....

Yogurt, plain:
partially skim milk, 8-oz. container ....
whole milk, 8-oz. container ....

This Cookbook is a perfect gift for Holidays, Weddings, Anniversaries & Birthdays.

To order extra copies as gifts for your friends, please use Order Forms on reverse side of this page.

* * * * * * * * * *

Cookbook Publishers, Inc. has published millions of personalized cook-books for every kind of organization from every state in the union. We are pleased to have the privilege of publishing this fine cookbook.

ORDER FORM

Use the order forms below for obtaining
additional copies of this cookbook.

Fill in Order Forms Below - Cut Out and Mail

You may order as many copies of our Cookbook as you wish for the regular price, plus $2.50 postage and packing per book ordered. Mail to:

**John S. Malone
Building 5, Apartment 2F
11811 Ave. of PGA
Palm Beach Gardens, FL 33418**

Please mail _____ copies of your Cookbook @ $10.00 each, plus $2.50 postage and packing per book ordered.

Mail books to:

Name _____

Address _____

City, State, Zip _____

You may order as many copies of our Cookbook as you wish for the regular price, plus $2.50 postage and packing per book ordered. Mail to:

**John S. Malone
Building 5, Apartment 2F
11811 Ave. of PGA
Palm Beach Gardens, FL 33418**

Please mail _____ copies of your Cookbook @ $10.00 each, plus $2.50 postage and packing per book ordered.

Mail books to:

Name _____

Address _____

City, State, Zip _____

COOK UP A
FUNDRAISING SUCCESS!

You Collect the Recipes *and* We do the Rest!

We have helped thousands of groups like yours,
so let us show you how easy it is to create a successful cookbook.

The following features are included in your cookbook at no additional charge:

* **Washable
  Full-Color Covers**

* **Seven Full-Color
  Divider Pages**

* **Professional
  Typesetting**
  of recipe pages—
  not typewritten

* **Three Pages
  to Print Information**
  about your organization

* **Table of Contents
  & Alphabetized
  Recipe Index**

* **Coupon Page** to help you
  sell your cookbooks

* **Colorful Full Length
  Plastic Ring Binders**
  allowing book to lie flat
  while in use

* **We Pay the Freight
  with FREE Cookbooks**
  on every order

Send Coupon below or Call TOLL-FREE 1-800-227-7282

We Can Create a Cookbook For You Too!

Our Fundraising Personalized Cookbook Program is Fun, Easy, AND Profitable!

You furnish the recipes—and we do the rest! We even supply you with FREE recipe forms!! Your organization's name can be on the front cover of your very own cookbook. AND the names of the recipe contributors appear with their submitted recipes.

YOUR BOOKS ARE SELF-FINANCING
You figure the cost of your books from our Price Chart. Costs are based on the number of recipes you want printed and the number of books you want to order.

NO DOWN PAYMENT
NO INTEREST OR HANDLING CHARGES
One-half of balance 37 days after books are shipped—remaining balance, 67 days after books are shipped. Thirty-day extension on written request if needed (making a total of 97 days).

For your FREE Step-by-Step Personalized Cookbook Instruction Kit return the postage-paid card today or call toll-free
1-800-227-7282

 Interested in additional fundraising ideas? Just ask us about our other fundraising programs when you call, or simply check the appropriate box on the opposite side of the business reply card shown below, then drop the card in the mail today.

(Tear along perforation, fill in reverse side and mail)